Strategic Information Management

CHANDOS
INFORMATION PROFESSIONAL SERIES

Series Editor: Ruth Rikowski
(email: Rikowskigr@aol.com)

Chandos' new series of books are aimed at the busy information professional. They have been specially commissioned to provide the reader with an authoritative view of current thinking. They are designed to provide easy-to-read and (most importantly) practical coverage of topics that are of interest to librarians and other information professionals. If you would like a full listing of current and forthcoming titles, please visit our website www.chandospublishing.com or contact Hannah Grace-Williams on email info@chandospublishing.com or telephone number +44 (0) 1993 848726.

New authors: we are always pleased to receive ideas for new titles; if you would like to write a book for Chandos, please contact Dr Glyn Jones on email gjones@chandospublishing.com or telephone number +44 (0) 1993 848726.

Bulk orders: some organisations buy a number of copies of our books. If you are interested in doing this, we would be pleased to discuss a discount. Please contact Hannah Grace-Williams on email info@chandospublishing.com or telephone number +44 (0) 1993 848726.

Strategic Information Management: A practitioner's guide

JELA WEBB

Chandos Publishing

Oxford · England

Chandos Publishing (Oxford) Limited
TBAC Business Centre
Avenue 4
Station Lane
Witney
Oxford OX28 4BN
UK
Tel: +44 (0) 1993 848726 Fax: +44 (0) 1865 884448
Email: info@chandospublishing.com
www.chandospublishing.com

First published in Great Britain in 2008

ISBN:
978 1 84334 376 9 (paperback)
978 1 84334 377 6 (hardback)
1 84334 376 2 (paperback)
1 84334 377 0 (hardback)

© J. Webb, 2008

British Library Cataloguing-in-Publication Data.
A catalogue record for this book is available from the British Library.

Typeset by Domex e-Data Pvt. Ltd.
Printed in the UK and USA.

Contents

List of figures, tables and boxes

Figures

Tables

Boxes

About the author

Jela Webb first became interested in the concepts associated with information and knowledge management (IKM) in the late 1990s while doing research for her MBA dissertation examining teamwork in organisations. This led to a role heading the knowledge management team in a major UK bank, where her responsibilities included the promotion of learning technologies and the development of knowledge management tools and techniques to help the organisation understand, capture and make use of its intellectual assets.

In 2000 she left the bank to form her own business, Azione Consulting, offering a range of strategic advisory services to organisations wishing to implement and develop their own IKM agendas.

One of the first people in Europe to be awarded an MSc in Information and Knowledge Management, Jela is also a visiting Lecturer at two UK universities, Brighton and London Metropolitan, and at Regent's Business School, London.

Jela has written articles and reports on IKM and related topics for a range of publications and has presented at conferences both in the UK and abroad. She has also been involved in research programmes focusing on skills for the 'information and knowledge economy'.

Jela may be contacted at: *jela.webb@azione.co.uk*.

List of abbreviations

AIIP	Association of Independent Information Professionals
ALA	American Library Association
ARMA	American Records Management Association
ASLIB	The Association for Information Managment
BPR	business process re-engineering
BRIC	Brazil, Russia, India and China
CILIP	Chartered Institute of Library and Information Professionals
CIO	chief information officer
CRM	customer relationship management
CSF	critical success factor
EDM	electronic document management
FAQ	frequently asked question
FOI	Freedom of Information
FSA	Financial Services Authority
FTP	file transfer protocol
HPA	Health Protection Agency
ICT	information and communication technology
IIMA	International Information Management Association
IKM	information and knowledge management
IM	information management
IP	internet protocol
IRR	internal rate of return
ISO	International Organization for Standardization

IT	information technology
KPI	key performance indicator
QC	quality circle
R&D	research and development
RM	records management
SEC	Securities and Exchange Commission
ROI	return on investment
SLA	service level agreement
STEEPLE	sociocultural, technological, economical, environmental, political, legal and ethical
SWOT	strengths, weaknesses, opportunities and threats
TQM	total quality management
URL	uniform resource locator

Introduction

This book is based on my experiences both of teaching Strategic Information Management and of the practical implementation of information management strategies and policies within organisational settings.

I first became involved with the concept of information and knowledge management in 1998 when I was completing my MBA dissertation on team working within organisations. My research, based on a case study undertaken in the organisation where I was then employed, provided a good deal of evidence of 'silo thinking' and 'silo working'[1] and not much evidence of collaboration and cooperation between the various business units. Sharing of information (and indeed knowledge) was not really very high on the organisational agenda and there was very little by way of formal information management strategies.

My organisation was by no means alone in this; the idea that information is a real business asset that requires careful management had not yet received the attention that it so obviously deserved. In consequence, by omitting to think specifically about how to manage a key asset – information – many organisations were failing to reach their full potential.

I was subsequently appointed to a senior position with responsibility for rolling out an information and knowledge management programme, a challenge that I accepted wholeheartedly, and I spent two very enjoyable years getting to grips with all that it entailed. During this time I began to receive requests from other organisations to help them with their information strategies, to participate in national and international research programmes in related areas, to contribute to the growing literature in the field and to present at conferences both in the UK and abroad.

My personal development path took me down the route of studying for an MSc in Information and Knowledge Management and I was one of the first students to receive this award. I was subsequently asked to share my experiences and to teach on the programme, and since 2003 I have been the Module Leader for Strategic Information Management at London Metropolitan University. I also teach related topics at the University of Brighton and Regent's Business School in London.

In 2000, I left full-time employment to set up my own information and knowledge management consultancy, Azione. Drawing on my experiences as a practitioner and as an academic in this exciting area, I am still finding that many organisations are struggling to come to terms with how fundamental good information management is to business success. They are failing to maximise the value of their information assets. My aim in writing this book is to provide a very practical guide and to take the reader, in a step-by-step process, through the key issues, as I see them, that should be considered if good information management is to become embedded in their organisation.

While the content is based very much on the subjects I promote to my students, I have adapted my presentation so that the book is very much a practitioner's guide, designed as an aid for anyone charged with responsibility for managing organisational information.

In the Appendix you will find a Toolkit that draws on material presented in the book and aims to provide practical assistance in the form of development activities, templates and exercises. These have been designed to help you to enhance your strategic information management skills.

You can determine the speed at which you work through the Toolkit. You may feel that you need to develop some areas quickly or to complete a particular activity so as to meet a deadline. Other areas may be 'nice to do' rather than 'need to do', and so may not be quite so pressing. Ultimately, the way in which you use the Toolkit will depend on your own personal circumstances: take from it the parts that you feel will be really useful to you as you either embark on or continue the journey to making strategic information management a reality in your organisation.

Note

1. The terms 'silo thinking' and 'silo working' describe parts of an organisation thinking and working in a stand-alone manner and not integrating their activities with other parts of the organisation.

Strategic awareness

Strategy is necessary in all organisations. Increased global competition in the private sector and continued pressure for resources in the public sector are leading to a broader recognition of the need for all managers to be strategically aware. The ability to think strategically is a key competence. If an organisation is to be successful, all employees must understand the business, what it is trying to achieve, what their particular role is and how they are contributing on a day-to-day basis to helping the organisation to fulfil its strategy.

An overview of strategy

When we talk about 'strategic information management' it is important first to understand what is meant by referring to it as 'strategic'. This chapter will provide an overview of strategy that will ensure from the outset that we think consistently with regard to the relationship between organisational strategy and information management activity. By the end of this chapter you will have developed strategic awareness. Later on in the book we will consider strategy formulation for information management in greater depth.

The dictionary defines strategy as 'the art of guiding, forming or carrying out a plan'. Whatever your role in an organisation, you are highly likely to be on the receiving end of organisational strategy. What does strategy mean to you?

You may say that it means any one or a combination of the following:

- objectives – short/medium/long
- targets
- success
- guidelines to work to
- establishing 'where are we now?'
- competitive advantage
- pulling together.

Let's take each of these in turn.

Objectives – short/medium/long

Organisations set themselves objectives that need to be achieved in order to satisfy their stakeholders (internal and external). By achieving the objectives an organisation can measure how successful it has been in a strategic sense. Objectives, by their nature, are high level and need to be broken down into ambitious, achievable and manageable targets.

Targets

Targets follow on from objectives and measure the achievement of objectives. They can be and are cascaded down through the organisation, driving the right behaviours and ensuring consistency of activities. Information managers, for example, will ensure that their activities reflect and support the organisational objectives. Indeed, if information managers do not ensure that their activities (and those for which they are responsible) underpin the wider organisational strategies, there is a risk that the information management programme will fail to deliver its intended goals.

Success

What is success? What does success mean to the organisation? In the dynamic information economy,[1] what may be regarded as a success in the short term may be quite different from success in the long term. It is essential to measure progress at periodic intervals. Remain alive to the need to change your view of 'what success means to us' as both internal and external forces determine new activities.

Critical Success Factors (CSFs) are those things that are essential to success, those things that drive the business. Once they have been identified, consideration can be given to how they will be measured. These measures are called Key Performance Indicators (KPIs). Each CSF must have at least one KPI, otherwise those business clichés such as 'what doesn't get managed doesn't get measured' and 'if you don't manage it, you can't improve it' become reality.

Guidelines to work to

While many job descriptions in organisations do not include the word 'strategy', this does not mean that employees are not expected to help achieve the strategy. People at all levels are expected to think and act strategically. Building strategic awareness in the organisation includes setting work guidelines that enable everyone to know that they are helping to achieve the broader organisational strategy. Being able to see how their own efforts are contributing will undoubtedly help employees to 'buy in' to the broader strategy.

Where are we now?

Strategy development starts with understanding where the organisation is now and reviewing its recent achievements, so that it can be realistic in setting new objectives. It is then appropriate to ask 'Where do we want to be?' and 'How will we get there?' All this must be based on a realistic understanding of the internal and external environment in which the organisation operates, how the environments may change and what capabilities the organisation has or needs in order to be able to respond effectively to any change in those environments.

Competitive advantage

Organisations achieve competitive advantage by giving their customers what they need or want, and by doing so more effectively than their competitors and in ways that are difficult for their competitors to replicate. What sets your organisation apart from the competition? What is it particularly adept at? In the specific context of information management, information (and knowledge) is increasingly being recognised as a source of competitive advantage. Business leaders are demanding information to support key business drivers such as improved productivity, getting new products and services to market faster than the competition, increasing customer loyalty through high service levels, and increasing market penetration.

Pulling together

'Pulling together' means the people in the organisation working together to achieve the overall strategy; helping employees to work together and to agree on what they should be achieving; and ensuring that they are not pulling in conflicting directions. How does information management support any behaviour and culture changes that are needed to facilitate greater team working? It does so by removing barriers to the sharing of information between different business units and by encouraging positive action through building communities of good practice and innovation.

Strategic awareness comes from adopting a strategic perspective of all organisational functions, understanding the nature of the organisational strategy and, in effect, turning strategy into action; that is, seeing how and where your individual activities (actions) contribute to the achievement of the broader organisational strategy.

Strategic awareness also involves constant scanning of the internal and external business environments, understanding how those environments affect the business, and being responsive and flexible in terms of the strategic changes they may require. It also involves taking a bird's-eye view by rising above the day-to-day operational detail and, of course, balancing near- and long-term opportunities and issues.

What is strategy?

If we take a few minutes to reflect upon what we have said so far, and on the words and phrases used, we could say that, in very simple terms, strategy can be defined as:

- knowing where you are
- knowing where you want to be
- knowing how to get there.

However, nothing is quite that simple. Strategy is a broad and complex subject that has given rise to a wealth of literature; many writers, consultants and practitioners have tried to address this multifaceted subject by designing tools and frameworks. In spite of this, there is no simple solution to strategy – if there were, every organisation would be devising and following a successful strategy.

The nature of competition and increasing globalisation of markets means that following a standard process will not result in sustainable strategic success. That said, organisations do make use of strategic frameworks and models to help address and meet strategic challenges. The point is not to use too many, to be selective and to make sure that you understand their purpose and how they can assist and, importantly, what their limitations may be. If they're right for your organisation, then adapt and modify them to ensure a better fit with your specific circumstances. Don't be railroaded into taking them at face value; always ask 'So what does this mean?' Remain open in your thinking, canvass the views of colleagues, particularly those who challenge your view and, importantly, always leave room for creativity and innovation.

The purpose of this book is not to make you a strategy expert but to help you to understand the basics of strategy and some of the tools used in strategy formulation, and to assist you to develop strategic awareness. Thus you, as an information professional, will be able to understand some basic strategic planning processes that will help you to see how information management strategy can be aligned with the broader organisational strategy. It will help you to ensure that the information management strategy is a key component of organisational strategy.

Lets us look in a little more depth at our simple definition of strategy.

Knowing where you are

This is about knowing and understanding

- the business you are in; the environment, internal and external, local, national and global
- who your customers are

- who your competitors are
- what is happening in your market
- what the economic outlook is
- how attractive your sector/industry is
- your competitive position
- your strengths, weaknesses, opportunities and threats.

Knowing where you want to be

This is about knowing and understanding

- the organisation's mission
- which sector or industry you want to be in
- what your source of competitive advantage will be
- how you can grow/expand your business
- what your success criteria will be.

Knowing how to get there

This is about knowing and understanding

- what actions you need to take
- what the resource implications are
- whether your organisation is aligned to deliver the strategy
- how the strategy will be communicated
- how to get full employee buy-in
- what things the organisation needs to change
- how the organisation will develop the flexibility to change
- how it will make those changes.

A key role of the information management department should be to improve the organisation's effectiveness by providing all employees with information at the right time so as to enable them to carry out their responsibilities as effectively as possible; that is, by having the right information available, at the right time, in the right place, in the right format and to the right people.

Strategic planning

Strategic planning should happen throughout the organisation, starting with the top-level managers, who in turn cascade the objectives down to lower levels until each employee has a set of objectives to achieve. In doing this, the organisation ensures that everyone is working in a coordinated way and fulfilling the strategy of the top level.

In larger organisations, which can be complex and diverse, there may be a number of different strategy levels. An example could be along the following lines:

1 Corporate (top-level) strategy

At this level strategy is concerned with the overall purpose and scope of the organisation: establishing the mission and meeting the expectations of stakeholders.

2 Business unit strategy

This follows on from the corporate strategy and is the strategy of a single, self-contained business unit, which could be a large or small unit, an autonomous unit, a division, or a profit centre with its own customers, income and competitors. The information management department will formulate its business unit strategy to fit in with the (higher-level) corporate strategy.

3 Operational strategy

This is concerned with how the component parts of the organisation, in terms of resources, processes, people and skills, will deliver the corporate and business unit strategies.

4 Product strategy

In some organisations there will also be a product strategy, focusing on competition in individual markets, geographical areas and specific product groups.

Strategic tools and frameworks

To help with strategy formulation, organisations use tools and frameworks to perform analysis in a structured manner. In this section we will provide an overview of the most commonly used strategic tools and frameworks:

- SWOT analysis
- STEEPLE analysis
- Porter's Five Forces analysis
- Scenario analysis.

SWOT analysis

SWOT analysis is probably the best-known strategic tool and is used in 80 per cent of organisations. SWOT stands for Strengths, Weaknesses, Opportunities and Threats. Undertaking a SWOT analysis involves describing the organisation's internal capabilities (strengths and weaknesses) in relation to the opportunities and threats from its competitive environment. It is a helpful way of classifying the issues faced by the organisation, although sometimes it can be difficult to distinguish whether a particular issue is strength or a weakness. However, the most important thing is to identify internal and external strategic factors and to understand their implications, rather than to become bogged down with classification. SWOT is a snapshot in time, and actions must be taken to achieve ongoing beneficial results.

- *Strengths*. These are the internal characteristics of the organisation that have a positive effect on its current and/or longer-term position. What is the organisation is good at? What (competitive) advantages does the organisation have that it can exploit?

- *Weaknesses*. These are also internal characteristics. What impedes the achievement of goals? What do your competitors do better than you? What areas does the organisation need to develop? Which areas attract the most negative feedback from customers?

- *Opportunities*. These are features of the external environment that the organisation may or should be able to exploit to its advantage.

- *Threats*. These also relate to the external environment. What might happen in the external environment to put you at a disadvantage and hinder your competitive position?

SWOT analysis helps to identify strategic aims and where the focus should be. The underlying aim should be to preserve and sustain opportunities, offset weaknesses, exploit opportunities and reduce threats.

STEEPLE analysis

This acronym stands for Sociocultural, Technological, Economical, Environmental, Political, Legal and Ethical.

STEEPLE analysis is often used in conjunction with a SWOT analysis.

A STEEPLE analysis is a simple checklist for reviewing the impact on the organisation of the current and future business environment and of global developments such as the emergence of the BRIC (Brazil, Russia, India and China) economies as major economic powers.

Factors are identified under the following headings:

- *Sociocultural.* Demographic trends, work/life balance, job security, employability, income trends, education, fashions, mobility, living conditions, poverty levels.

- *Technological.* IT spend, new communication channels, R&D spend, speed of technology transfer, social networking trends, technology innovations and rates of obsolescence, internet.

- *Economical.* Global economy, emergence of developing countries as major forces of economic power, economic cycles, inflation, interest rates, exchange rates, EU expansion, unemployment, oil prices.

- *Environmental.* Climate change, global warming, recycling, organic farming and food, green issues, carbon footprint, carbon trading, Kyoto Treaty (reducing emissions).

- *Political.* Government, election results, White Papers, Competition Commission, fiscal policies, UN sanctions.

- *Legal.* Legislation: employment law, discrimination legislation, green laws, health and safety, data protection, freedom of information, minimum wage, working hours directives.

- *Ethical.* Ethical and moral standards, codes of conduct, cross-cultural working, client confidentiality, business ethics, consent, Official Secrets Act, security access, terms of business/trade, trust, reputation.

Porter's Five Forces analysis

Michael Porter is a thought leader and is regarded as one of the most influential writers on strategy. In his book *Competitive Strategy* (Porter, 1980), he offered the 'Five Forces' model as a way of understanding the forces that shape strategies within industries. Although the book was published over 25 years ago, it is nonetheless required reading for students of business strategy and Porter's Five Forces model is still widely used as a strategic analysis tool.

Porter argued that there are five forces shaping strategy within industries:

1 Rivalry among firms

2 Threat of substitute products

3 Threat of new entrants

4 Bargaining power of suppliers

5 Bargaining power of buyers.

The model is often presented as shown in Figure 1.1.

The relative strengths of these five forces determine the profitability of the industry (industry is defined as a grouping of firms that market products that are a close substitute for each other, e.g., the computer industry, the mobile phone industry, the airline industry). Porter states that an organisation needs to understand these five forces and then adopt a position from which to defend itself against them and to influence the factors in its favour.

He goes on to state that there are only three strategic options available:

1 Differentiation: make your offering such that it is perceived as being unique and different from the rest of the industry.

Figure 1.1   Michael Porter's Five Forces model

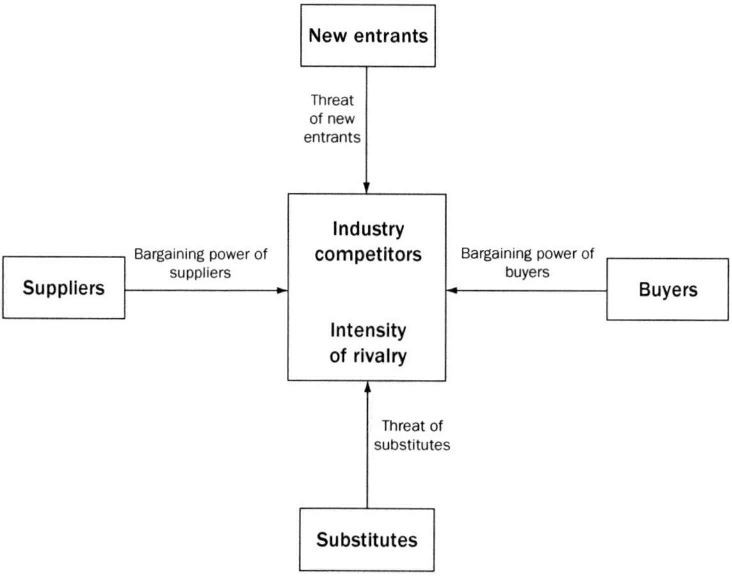

Source: Porter (1990).

2 Cost leadership: sell on price, but with such tight controls that you are profitable.

3 Focus: deal only in a specific market or geographic location.

According to Porter, failure to follow one of these three options will leave the organisation struggling 'somewhere in the middle'.

Scenario analysis

Scenario analysis is a model for learning about the future. It takes frameworks such as STEEPLE a stage further and, after prioritising the key issues, considers the possible scenarios for some of the external influences. In scenario analysis a list of probable impacts is drawn up and then assessed as to whether each is insignificant, inevitable or critically uncertain. It is the 'critically uncertain' issues for which action plans need to be developed.

Drawing up a small number of scenarios – stories of how the future may unfold – is the basis of corporate strategy. It is important to try to keep them relatively simple. Scenarios should stimulate debate, challenge current business thinking and help decision makers to think more strategically.

It is important to remember that scenarios address uncertainty and help the organisation to understand it. They are not a forecast and are only as good as the quality of the information on which they are based. They can be extremely time consuming, needing a lot of thought and attention, and should be monitored, evaluated and reviewed regularly.

One of the first organisations to use scenario analysis was Shell, the global oil, gas and petrochemical company. In the 1970s it constructed a scenario for the potential effects of a fall in the oil price (unthinkable at the time). When the price of oil did subsequently fall, Shell was in the position of knowing what actions to take and fared much better than its competitors in dealing with the energy crisis of 1973, the price shock of 1979 and the collapse of the oil market in the mid 1980s.

Strategic awareness for information professionals

Organisations make extensive use of strategic tools and frameworks. There are many available and we have only scratched the surface in presenting four commonly used ones. It is recommended that you find out which ones are used in your organisation. Study them carefully, as this will help you to understand the business, the challenges faced by the organisation and how and where information management can help the organisation to fulfil its strategy. Becoming strategically aware will enable you to consider the strategic value of the organisation's information (which you are responsible for managing), to raise your profile and to show how valuable information is and how important it is for it to be managed strategically.

Becoming strategically aware involves 'big picture' thinking and appreciating interdependencies throughout the organisation. For example, how does information management affect the different parts of the business such as research and development, marketing, human resources, product development?

Managing information strategically should be no different from strategically managing what we regard as more traditional assets, such as finances, human resources, property and so forth. It starts with becoming strategically aware and continues with developing strategic thinking skills and developing a strategic plan for information management, implementing the strategy and measuring its effectiveness.

Once information professionals become strategically aware, they become able to see how they can make a difference to the organisation by highlighting how information can and should be managed to help meet the organisation's strategic goals. They recognise the role that information management has to play in the organisational context and how information can be used to create a more effective and efficient organisation. They recognise how information resources can be positioned to help fulfil the organisation's strategic objectives. This, in turn, will raise the profile of information management.

Information management strategy and corporate strategy are increasingly interdependent. Information strategy must be formulated in the context of corporate strategy. Equally, a corporate strategy that has been developed without consideration of the opportunities presented by the strategic use of information may be seriously deficient: information is the lifeblood of many organisations. Thus, information professionals are placed at the heart of the business and must develop an awareness of the broader strategic management issues in the organisation. This will ensure that proper account is taken of strategic information management issues when the broader corporate strategy is being developed.

In today's fast-paced economies, there is little doubt as to the importance of information: it is mission critical. There are very few, if any, organisations that do not need good information management in order to succeed. Good strategic information management will ensure that information is seen for what it is: a valuable asset, something that should be prized, used and respected.

Good information professionals, who understand the business, are forward thinking and strategically aware and have a key role to play in supporting the organisation to achieve its objectives and succeed in the marketplace, whether in the private or the public sector.

Summary

In this chapter we have considered what is meant by 'strategy' and examined a few of the most commonly used tools and frameworks for strategy formulation. One of the most challenging aspects of strategy is its scope; there is a wealth of literature available on the topic, but here we have sought to help you, the information professional, to develop strategic awareness and thus raise the profile of information management in your organisation.

Toolkit activity

- Activity 1: Developing strategic awareness
- Activity 2: SWOT template
- Activity 3: STEEPLE exercise

Note

1. An economy in which the emphasis is on information as a source of wealth creation. It is not solely related to the increasing capability of technology to enhance performance, but also stresses innovation as a core capability of organisational performance.

2

Defining information management

Development of information management

Information management (IM) as a discipline is relatively new, having emerged during the 1990s, but activities associated with IM can be traced back to the earliest of civilisations.

Before the development of writing, information was transmitted orally; because oral transmission relied on the memory, facts and themes were often distorted as they were passed from one person to another. Preserving the original version, which was so important to the development of knowledge about the world, did not occur until the invention of writing about 4,000 years ago.

We know, from the discovery of ancient cuneiform scripts in Syria dating back to about 2300 BC, that attempts were made to record details of commercial transactions, law-making processes and the social order so that this information could easily be passed from one generation to the next. However, they were of very little use for preserving lengthy information, as the writing method – incising words on clay tablets – was not conducive to recording anything other than fairly short texts.

It was not until the development of papyrus, an early form of paper, in Egypt, that it became possible to easily record and transport the literary and academic works of the day. Papyrus was later replaced by parchment, but both were susceptible to destruction by fire.

The establishment of the libraries of antiquity, most notably the library of Alexandria, founded in 3 BC and which lasted for a thousand years, provides early examples of information management. The library at Alexandria had a vast collection of works, covered very diverse subjects, had a reputation as a centre for research and learning and was primarily used as such by students of many different disciplines. It was said to contain over 500,000 written works in the form of books and scrolls. Copies of its books and scrolls (information) were made and circulated throughout the (known) world. Invading armies later destroyed the contents of the library by setting fire to it. Archaeological excavations have indicated that it could accommodate up to 5,000 students at any one time.

With the passing of ancient civilisations, attempts were made to preserve information and knowledge gained through experience and reflection, and much of the knowledge of the ancient Greeks and Persians was preserved in Arabic translations. These works, in time, found their way to the European monasteries, where monks translated them so that they would be available to non-Arabic-speaking scholars. The skills of information and library sciences can probably be traced back to this time. The work was laborious, all done by hand, and once again in a medium that was not that easily transportable.

A significant breakthrough came with the invention of the printing press, which allowed information to be disseminated to a much wider audience than hitherto. While the printing process was limited to those who could use the 'new technology', production and dissemination were enhanced and print began to replace the previously oral traditions as the major means of information distribution.

In the twentieth century, electronic information and communication technologies (ICTs) have facilitated the capture, storage and dissemination of information, and at speeds unimaginable by earlier generations. Information is now easily accessible, across time zones and geographical boundaries. ICTs have increased the pace of change in the that way organisations operate and in the roles that employees occupy. They demand new patterns of work and affect the nature of individual jobs and the structure of work groups. As electronic technologies continue to evolve, we see organisations able to communicate around the clock, collaborate virtually and share information both synchronously and asynchronously. Sophisticated information management techniques are driving competitive advantage.

There can be little doubt that the complexities of twenty-first-century working differentiate information management from the challenges faced by ancient civilisations or the medieval monasteries: globalisation, technology, language and communications. Information is all pervasive; the volume of information, both internal and external, continues to grow apace. The concept of 'information overload' is real, with information in all its formats being pushed and pulled by diverse audiences for a variety of purposes. Ensuring that information is harnessed effectively and deployed intelligently is a major challenge for today's organisations.

As stated above, IM emerged as a management discipline since the 1990s. While this is not always explicitly stated, it followed organisational initiatives such as quality circles (QCs), total quality management (TQM) and business process re-engineering (BPR). These initiatives should not be discounted as fads: they all challenged organisations to think about the way they operated, how they were structured and how they behaved. All had an impact on IM practice. It is important to appreciate the seeds sown by such initiatives in driving forward information management practices.

Quality circles

QCs were formed by small groups of employees who met regularly to identify, analyse, discuss and solve work-related issues – quality, productivity or other concerns – using problem-solving techniques. The proposed solutions were presented to management and the QCs themselves were involved in the implementation of new processes and procedures.

Total quality management

TQM was a top-down initiative that sought to improve processes and procedures in order to enhance customer satisfaction. It placed strong emphasis on good and visionary leadership, with management being responsible for initiating change. TQM operated on the basis of continuous processes of improvement, but the empowerment of workers was often restricted by the boundaries set by management.

Business process re-engineering

BPR looked at business processes and investigated the complete restructuring of organisations, streamlining and often cutting out layers of management – ultimately achieving significant improvements in organisational processes.

What is the relationship between information management and these initiatives? At their centre was a concern with organisational processes and how they could lead to improved customer satisfaction and give competitive edge. None of the improvements could have been achieved without the effective use of information. By highlighting unnecessary or duplicated activities they were able to assess how they were currently operating and analyse what needed to be changed so as to realise efficiencies through streamlining (future) activities. Good management of information was at the heart of many successful projects.

Definition of information management

What do we mean when we talk about 'information management'?

Information management is the process by which information

- is identified, created, stored, used and shared efficiently and effectively as part of day-to-day organisational processes

- flows effectively throughout the organisation, so that all employees have easy access to relevant information, when they need it

- is used responsibly, with due regard for its classification and regulation as well as the compliance issues surrounding information holdings

- is regarded as a key organisational asset that is managed strategically, in the same manner as more traditional assets, such as land, labour and capital

- is viewed as a currency of competition

- is prized and respected.

Let us pause and consider how we define information. A simple means to help us is to consider 'information' as part of the continuum often presented in the literature as:

Data → Information → Knowledge

- *Data* are the raw facts, a series of discrete observations and measurements which in themselves do not reveal a great deal. Often stored in a technology system, data are made easily accessible to employees through wide use of networking technologies.

- *Information* is a message constituted and analysed from the data in a way that gives it meaning and allows it to be understood. It may be in the form of a document or in audio or visual formats.

- *Knowledge* is information that is placed in context, based on insight and experience. Knowledge may be explicit, in that it can be formal, written, systematic and recorded in words, pictures or repositories or embodied in practices and procedures; it may also be tacit, that is, informal, residing in people's heads as insights, intuition, judgement or skills, and therefore difficult to formalise and articulate.

Data, information and knowledge are terms often used interchangeably by organisations, but it is useful to make the distinction so as to avoid misunderstanding. In the context of this book, information is regarded as that which is generated internally as well as that obtained from external sources. It is generally believed that 80 per cent of the information needed by employees to do their jobs effectively is internally generated and that the remaining 20 per cent comes from external sources.

From the late 1980s onwards awareness emerged in organisations across many sectors that much value and opportunity might lie in giving greater importance to information management issues. Organisations began to appreciate that information was a key asset which, if managed properly, could improve operations, facilitate efficiency and effectiveness, and provide competitive advantage.

Information management initiatives

One of the common misconceptions about information management is that it is solely about records management; or electronic document management; or the intranet; or customer relationship management. Too often, and especially in the early days, there was a tendency to view information management as a technology issue, concentrating disproportionately on the technology to the detriment of a human-centred approach. Technology should be regarded as an enabler of information management, rather than a driver.

Records management (RM)

Records management is concerned with the creation, storage, maintenance, use and disposal of records, often hard-copy records in the form of documents, but also in the form of artefacts or other media. Organisations create records which contain information; part of the records management process involves making sure that available information is kept up to date and that information that has reached its 'sell by' date is archived or disposed of. Understanding who is responsible for which records in an organisation is also important.

Electronic document management (EDM)

EDM functions as for records management, but focuses on electronic documents (records). With the technologies now available to organisations, it is important to be able to manage effectively the vast array of electronic documents that are being created and stored. Indexing and classifying documents for ease of identification and use forms part of an EDM strategy.

Intranets

Intranets use the technology of the web to share information internally between employees. A good intranet strategy will ensure that an organisation is really using and exploiting the potential inherent in its information assets. By harnessing technologies effectively, a well-designed and executed intranet can provide possibilities far beyond the creation of and access to information: it can encourage the development of a culture where information sharing becomes the norm, provide an effective communication channel and contribute widely to organisational learning and innovation. An effective intranet will ensure that information is easily accessible to all employees.

Customer relationship management (CRM)

A CRM program uses technology to bring together all the information about the customer base and its interactions with the organisation and can also demonstrate where future developments should be focused. Customers interact with organisations in a variety of ways, including one-to-one contact (e.g., face-to-face, telephone, text messaging), through call-centres, via the internet, through mail order and by interactive methods such as e-mail or SMS. A strategy that encourages two-way communication with the customer, regardless of the range of channels used, captures valuable information and ensures that the organisation gains a thorough understanding of the ways in which customers behave, what their requirements are, how profitable they are and what the organisation needs to do in order to remain the 'first choice' of the existing customer base and to attract new customers in a very competitive environment.

Technology and information

Technology has a significant role to play in good information management and should be viewed as the infrastructure that supports information management rather than as the complete answer to information management, as was the case in some first-generation initiatives. Too many information management initiatives failed to provide the anticipated benefits because it was thought that technology alone was the solution. Organisations using technology to help deliver information management should think about the way in which employees interact with information rather than how they interact with the technology. Much information that is used by employees isn't necessarily stored in electronic formats; employees obtain information from a variety of sources, and in many organisations the key source of information is other employees!

The idea that information is an asset that can be exploited to great effect poses many challenges and organisations have to think seriously about the range of information assets they hold, be they in intellectual property such as brands, patents and licences; business plans; procedural processes, rules and policies; business document templates and guidelines; customer, supplier and employee records; training manuals; business and competitor intelligence; product and service inventories; catalogues; registers; technical reports; financial records; ideas and so on. It is impossible to provide a comprehensive list, as each organisation will have its own range of information assets. This does, however, demonstrate the complexity involved in trying to identify both internal and external information assets.

If an organisation only focuses on one or two of the information management initiatives outlined above, it will not deliver effective information management. All of these initiatives, together with a due regard for the ways in which employees interact with information, have their part to play, and an integrated approach is the key to success.

It is interesting to note that, speaking at the World Economic Forum in 2000, the then British prime minister Tony Blair said: 'in an economy dominated by information and knowledge, education is king ... oil is no longer the most important commodity in the world: it is information'. He clearly saw information as the most important commodity in the economy.

The purpose of information management

Information management will mean different things to different organisations, and some would say that there is very little value in trying to offer a 'catch-all' definition. Each organisation should consider for itself how it should define information management. However, it is worth giving some thought to the purpose of information management, which will help with the definition and, at the very least, provide you with a starting-point for discussion and debate.

Strassman's definition

> The purpose of information management is to allocate, simplify, reduce costs, increase effectiveness and boost the quality of all information processes, whether or not they are automated. Information management includes co-ordinating suppliers, employees and customers in tasks including managing, training, counselling, co-ordinating, recording and reporting. It excludes physical production. (Strassman, 1995)

If we extract some principles from Strassman's definition we see that he advocates an integrated approach – involving all organisational stakeholders. He promotes strongly the aspect of 'inclusiveness', whereby all parts of the organisation are linked together, and goes on to argue that information management and information technology are supporting elements in business, functional and productivity planning. Information management should not be undertaken in isolation; an organisation needs to have a high level of information management competence if it is to be successful.

Fundamentally, if you are seeking to manage information, what you are aiming to do is to ensure that information that has been identified as being useful to the organisation can be accessed at the right time, in the right place, in the right formats and by the right people.

Aspects to be considered in this context are:

- *Right time* (availability). When is information available? How soon after creation should information be made available? Do employees have access to information to aid the decision-making process? Is it available 'just-in-time?'

- *Right place*. You need to consider storage issues and accessibility. Is information stored in hard copy and/or electronic repositories? How accessible are the various repositories? Is information stored on site or off site, or in a combination of the two? Has information storage been outsourced? Who has access?

- *Right format*. How do employees prefer to receive information – in hard copy, electronic formats? Is it up to date? Does the organisation have an information archiving policy?

- *Right people*. How do people work? Where do they work? Do you have a geographically distributed workforce? Are some employees home based? Have they the skills to be able to use information effectively? Which roles are particularly information intensive? Who is able to have access and what information security issues may you need to consider? Are all employees given access to everything, or not?

Critical success factors

In summary, an organisation needs to be clear as to what information it generates, holds and has access to. It needs to ensure that all information holdings, regardless of format, are organised for use. Employees who must or should be able to access and use information should have both the skills and the tools to access information efficiently and in formats that are meaningful in the situation that defines their need for access and use.

Information management involves and requires a clear understanding, at appropriate levels of the organisation, of the organisational structure and the processes that drive both core and peripheral functions. An understanding is needed of the relationship between tasks and processes, and how different parts of the organisation interact. Understanding the matrix of information relationships that exist across internal and external constituencies is essential. There is little point in trying to manage information is isolated pockets: information is interrelated and must be considered on a collective basis.

Information and communication technologies have their part to play, but should not be viewed as the whole solution to information management: they are tools that facilitate information management. A purely technology-centred approach to information management is to be avoided.

Experience has shown that good information management has many business benefits and that it should be considered as an ongoing management function that is as central to organisational operations as financial management and human resources management. Promote the idea that improvements in performance are more likely to emerge from appropriate information strategies and associated activities, and get others on board with your way of thinking.

Summary

In this chapter we have considered how information management has evolved to become a defined management discipline in its own right. We have seen some very early examples of information management dating back thousands of years and considered how late-twentieth-century organisational initiatives such as QCs, TQM and BPR forced organisations to examine the way they worked, and how these initiatives laid the groundwork for more formal information management processes.

We have also given some thought to other initiatives such as RM, EDM, CRM and intranets, which are sometimes regarded as providing information management *per se*, and have encouraged you to consider how important it is for such activities to be coordinated, rather than being implemented independently and without consistency.

We have considered the purpose of information management, which should give you a starting point for debate, and we have also highlighted some critical success factors.

Toolkit activity

- Activity 4: Defining information management

3

Information as an asset

Introduction

Many organisations recognise instinctively that information is
a key resource and that, in a business environment, information
is vital to ongoing success, whether that be in a profit-driven
enterprise or in the public or not-for-profit sectors.

The basis of wealth creation in today's economies has
moved to a position where information and knowledge, that is
to say, intangible assets, rather than tangible (physical) assets
account for the greater worth of a business. Economic wealth
is driven by the creation of information, by the manipulation
of information and by trading in information. Large parts of
the world economy are being driven by intangible assets – in
addition to information, one can quite easily assert that
knowledge, another intangible, also plays a key role.

Whether an organisation regards itself as a learning
organisation, as being at the forefront of creating new and
innovative products, or as harnessing the power of global
communications infrastructure, it is information and its use
by employees that enables it to compete successfully in its
chosen marketplace.

Consider for a moment the importance and value for a
pharmaceutical company developing a new drug of
information about the drug's potential side effects; or
information obtained by the intelligence services about

a proposed terrorist attack; or early notification to shareholders about a proposed company merger; and then think about the importance and value of information in your own organisation.

Is information given due recognition? Does your organisation fully understand what its information resources are? Does it manage information effectively or does it struggle to manage it? Does it appreciate that information is an asset that should be managed in the same way as physical assets (e.g., land, capital, labour, raw materials) are managed?

Information is all around us and we continue to see a significant increase in the volume of information we are expected to assimilate and act upon. Significant technological breakthroughs have increased accessibility to new channels of communication, sometimes so much so that an organisation can be said to be 'drowning in information'. Much of the concern and negativity around information lies in the fact that it is 'soft' and therefore not so easy to manage. Without recognition of its importance and in the absence of a proper information strategy, an organisation may fail to realise the full value of its information assets and consequently risk being overtaken by its competitors.

At the heart of good information management strategy is the need to treat information as an asset and to manage it, just like other assets.

The Hawley Report

The concept of 'information as an asset' was first articulated by the Hawley Committee, which was set up in the UK in 1994 under the chairmanship of Dr Robert Hawley, then Chief Executive of Nuclear Electric plc. The Hawley

Committee comprised a group of fifteen business executives from leading organisations, predominantly in the private and public sectors, whose remit was to try to establish a model for encouraging boards of directors to recognise the importance of information, to consider it a major asset and to take responsibility for its stewardship. While the Committee membership was UK focused, many of the organisations that participated in the research had an international reach.

Interviews were done in approximately forty organisations. The focus of the research was on the information assets of each organisation, the risks and opportunities relating to those assets and how they were dealt with, and on investigating the role of the board of directors (or its equivalent in the public sector) in setting information policies and monitoring related activities.

The Committee produced a report entitled *Information as an Asset – The Board Agenda* (The Hawley Committee, 1995), which created a great deal of interest in and understanding of the importance of information in organisational success and urged organisations to establish 'better policy and practices in relation to information assets'.

In recommending that information be defined as an asset, the Committee was working on the premise that 'every board of directors can relate to managing and reporting assets' and that therefore, by getting them to think of information as an asset, they would have a better understanding of information as a strategic resource that needed to be managed.

The Committee proposed that 'all significant information in an organisation, regardless of its purpose, should be properly identified, even if not in an accounting sense, for consideration as an asset of the business', and it recommended that the board of directors should make clear to management what actions it wished to be taken and who was responsible for action and compliance.

The report was important for a number of reasons:

- it moved forward the perception that information was a vital resource
- it identified information as a major organisational asset in its own right
- it considered information as an asset with a life cycle, starting with creation, followed by distribution, use and eventual disposal
- it defined board-level responsibilities for information (a radical move at the time)
- it highlighted the benefits of exploiting information assets
- it highlighted the consequences of not managing information assets effectively.

The Committee stated that the first step in exploiting the value of information was a formal identification process. Its research revealed that within organisations similar types of information were identified as being important and (possibly) strategic. Eight categories were defined, which were regarded as providing a useful starting point for those wishing to identify a list of information assets within their own organisation.

The eight categories are listed below, together with some examples that may assist you in considering what the information assets of your own organisation are.

Market and customer information

Information about customers. Who are our customers? Where are they located? What do we know about them? What issues are our customers facing? What type of services are they expecting from us? What are the trends in our customer-satisfaction surveys?

The following is an example of the type of market information that would be useful. If a retailer is thinking about expanding geographically and offering products and services in the developing world, it will need to look carefully at market information to assess whether the expansion strategy is viable. Keeping up to date via economic and market-research reports will be fundamental to developing the right strategy.

Another example would be that of a bank, which will hold significant amounts of data on each customer and can use this to predict when additional services may be appropriate. For example, the impending move of a customer to another part of the country might entail a need for a bridging loan for property purchase, a mortgage and/or assistance with relocation costs.

Product information

Good product information is essential to improving customer support and many organisations are focusing on improving the quality of their product information. One only needs to think of the expanding range of information that is now provided on food products, particularly in the context of the 'healthy eating' debate.

A company such as Dell, which sells computers online to a customer's own specification, has to provide good product information to enable the right choices to be made. This, in turn, provides a 'feel good' factor because customers perceive that they are receiving a highly personalised service.

Specialist knowledge

Specialist knowledge relates to the information required for operating in a particular area. For example, an insurance company wishing to diversify into marine insurance may well recruit an expert or even a whole team with many years' experience in the specialist field from a rival insurer. Tapping into their knowledge, which may well be tacit, and turning it into explicit knowledge will create a very valuable information asset.

Specialist knowledge may be tacit in that it resides in people's heads and is not explicitly articulated. The discipline that we now know as 'knowledge management' may well address this type of issue, but at the time when the Hawley Report was published, knowledge management was in its infancy.

Business process information

Business process information is concerned with the different activities required to produce a specific output for a customer or market. The emphasis is on how the work is done and in what sequence, one stage following another to reach the desired output. A simple example is the construction of a house, which starts with the foundations, then building the external and internal walls, roofing, plumbing, electrics, doors, windows and decoration, including fitting of kitchens and bathrooms.

Other types of business process information include the information that underpins the workings of a business, such as economic information, political information, and share price performance.

Business process information may also include templates for writing client proposals and submitting tenders, project management guidelines and information about procedures to be followed in the event of a breach of security.

Management information

This is information upon which major decisions will be based. Examples include monthly performance against targets and financial information (weekly, monthly or quarterly accounts).

Other types of regularly produced management information might include statistics, business intelligence and competitor intelligence.

Human resource information

Human resource information is vitally important for all businesses in the information economy and could include a wide variety of information relating to staff numbers, contact details, recruitment activity, payroll, staff turnover, training plans, staff appraisals and exit interviews.

In a business working very much on the basis of deploying project teams, a skills database would be very useful for matching up individuals with project requirements. A database detailing professional qualifications, languages spoken and expertise in specific areas of business activity would form part of human resource information.

Supplier information

Developing good relationships with suppliers will ensure that a business operates as effectively as possible by obtaining the best deals available, reducing delivery times and generally helping to improve customer service.

Information about supplier contracts and service-level agreements falls into this category. Prices, delivery times and information about the quality of goods and services purchased are important and should be reviewed regularly to ensure that your requirements are being met.

Information about contract reviews, proposed new suppliers or why an existing supplier's contract was terminated is relevant because it helps to inform future activity.

Accountable information

The type of information that falls into this category includes the legal and regulatory framework within which your business operates. Today's complex regulatory environment, including corporate governance codes, increasing legislation and compliance, places an increasing burden on organisations to demonstrate that they are complying with guidelines.

We have seen a growth in what many regard as 'red tape', but reporting on matters of compliance, government regulations and audit issues cannot be avoided. The better the information, the easier it is to provide evidence of compliance not only in relation to formal legislation but also in relation to less formal matters, such as ethical and moral issues faced in the business environment.

Each organisation will differ in what it regards as its information assets, and it is impossible to provide an exhaustive list of all the types of information assets that may fall into the categories mentioned above. When you consider the different types of information that are particularly important to your organisation, may you find that the categories specified in the Hawley Report need to be renamed so as to be more meaningful to your organisation's particular circumstances and activities. Similarly, you may find it easier to break down the categories even further and rather than, for example, bracketing together 'market and customer information', to view them as separate categories. Likewise, 'accountable information' may be better divided into externally and internally reportable areas.

A limitation of the categories specified by the Hawley Report is that the naming conventions have greater affinity to commercial, profit-driven businesses operating in the private sector than to the public and not-for-profit sectors. The public and not-for-profits sectors may have different information categories and will need to adapt descriptions best suited to their particular spheres of operation. However, it should not be too difficult to rename the categories so as to make them more relevant to particular operational circumstances.

Another point worth mentioning is that the Hawley Report focuses on internally generated information, whereas one must not overlook external information. The combination/integration of the two is needed for effective performance.

It is essential for organisations to recognise information (internal and external) as an asset, something that has value and can be used, just like more traditional assets, to help achieve an overall business strategy. Fortunately for the information professional, there is a growing realisation within business that information is a strategic resource, and this is helping to place it at the top of the organisational agenda.

Each organisation thus needs to develop an effective process for identifying its information assets and to produce an information asset register that is maintained and is subject to regular reviews. No one should pretend that this is an easy task; on the contrary, it can be quite a complex and time-consuming activity. However, without an understanding of its information assets an organisation will struggle to determine how these assets should best be managed, protected and used to advantage.

Organisations will inevitably take different approaches to the identification process and in the next chapter we will consider the integral role that an information audit plays.

Developing an agenda for managing information as an asset

All employees, from board level down, are aware of the importance of information in performing their roles. More and more of an employee's time is consumed by 'information work', which is integral to the vast majority of roles in the twenty-first-century organisation. Understanding what information is required in order for employees to do their jobs more effectively, and making that information accessible, in whatever format it is held, is a key goal for an organisation seeking to ensure that strategic information management becomes a reality.

The Hawley Report was very influential in getting organisations and, importantly, boards of directors, to recognise information as an asset that deserved the same care and attention as other organisational assets.

A board of directors has specific responsibilities, which include determining policies and strategies, monitoring performance, appointing senior management, accounting to shareholders and ensuring that the financial accounts accurately reflect the organisation's financial position. Legislation, shareholder agreements and articles of association cover their activities and, in certain circumstances a director who has not acted in accordance with regulations may be personally liable. Directors need to have the right information in order to perform their statutory duties and responsibilities effectively.

Some boards will require more information than others, and this will depend on the nature and complexity of the business. Whatever the size of the business, directors should ensure that they have the information they need to fulfil their responsibilities. Directors are responsible for ensuring that a company maintains full and accurate records, especially relating to its finances. They are expected to demonstrate a certain amount of skill and to exercise a duty of care in the way they go about their business. Information is a vital resource for them.

A board is usually made up of individuals who bring a variety of skills and expertise to the business, and while it is common for board members to be experienced in financial management, sales management, human resources management, typically they are less familiar with information management. As such, the board may need to devote more time to this aspect and ensure that it both seeks and obtains the right information.

In the Hawley Report is a ten-point agenda that provides a structure for developing good information management. The first three agenda items are directed to the board of directors and the remaining seven to the organisation.

The board

1 The first item focuses on the board satisfying itself that the information it uses is necessary and sufficient for its purpose.

2 This is about the board being aware of and properly advised on all the information aspects of the subjects on its agenda.

3 This concerns compliance with the law, regulations and ethics. It is particularly important for directors, as they can be made personally liable for any failure to comply with legislation and ignorance is not an acceptable defence.

The organisation

The seven items directed to the organisation form the structure of a policy for information management to be set by the board. The Hawley Report states that the board should determine the organisation's policy for information assets and identify how compliance with the policy will be measured and reviewed. It suggests the following activities:

4 This item relates to the identification of information assets and their classification into those assets that are of value and importance and merit special attention and those that do not.

This will involve drawing up a register of information assets and classifying them according to their importance and value to the business. Given the dynamic nature of the business environment, it is important to undertake regular reviews and to keep the information assets register up to date.

5 This item concerns the quality and quantity of information for effective operation, in order to ensure that, at every level, the information provided is necessary and sufficient, timely, reliable and consistent.

This reflects the need to ensure that the right information is available to the right people, at the right time and in the right format. It will require aspects such as knowing what information is available (e.g. the asset register), whether the information needed is available, whether the information is effective, whether the information is being processed properly, and thinking about control processes and how the organisation can establish an archiving policy to ensure that it is not working with out-of-date or obsolete information.

6 This item concerns proper use of information in accordance with legal and regulatory frameworks, operational and ethical standards, and the roles and responsibilities for the creation, safekeeping, access, change and destruction of information.

All businesses, regardless of geographical domicile, must comply with laws, but do they understand what the laws and regulations are regarding information? Businesses face an increasing number of compliance regulations and we regularly read stories about companies that have failed to conform to the latest compliance procedures. Forward-thinking organisations will ensure that they know what their compliance requirements are and will implement strategies to improve information management practices.

7 This item concerns the capability, suitability and training of people to safeguard and enhance information assets.

Do employee training programmes, starting from induction, include appropriate training in information management? Do employees fully understand their responsibilities with regard to information assets? What confidentiality agreements are in place?

8 This item concerns the protection of information from theft, loss, unauthorised access, abuse and misuse, including information that is the property of others.

Information security is a major concern for many organisations and is one of their biggest challenges. How do you protect information? Who decides who has access to what information? How do you deal with the increasing sophistication of cyber-related threats (viruses, spyware, Trojan horses and worms) and are you using protective measures such as anti-virus software, firewalls and anti-spam software?

9 This item concerns the harnessing of information assets and their proper use for the maximum benefit of the organisation, including legally protecting, licensing, reusing, combining, representing, publishing and destroying.

One way to achieve this is to have a policy whereby, when management is required to review organisational activities, standards, targets, etc., it makes a point of also reviewing information assets in these contexts.

10 The final item relates to the strategy for information systems, including those using computers and electronic communications, and the implementation of that strategy with particular reference to the costs, benefits and risks arising.

Typically, organisations will do this when they implement IT strategies, that is, they will ensure that the IT strategy is aligned with business strategy. However, they may not readily see that it should be no different when it comes to aligning information strategy with business strategy.

The Hawley agenda sought to provide a framework for the identification and management of information assets and, while it is now some years old, it nevertheless provides very useful guidance and has been used successfully in many organisations.

Implementing the Hawley agenda calls for top-level leadership, without which an organisation will surely invite failure. As with most change programmes, it is imperative that those in senior positions really champion the cause and demonstrate by deeds, not just by words, that they support the planned changes.

Recognising that information is an asset that needs careful management may be a challenge for some organisations, but if you are able to adapt the guidelines provided here and generate debate around the issues raised, you will be able to raise the profile of information and its importance for day-to-day operations.

The value of information

Creating an asset register will enable an organisation to see at a glance the full range of information assets (resources) it possesses and will quite possibly generate discussion as to the value of those assets. Information has numerous capabilities and differs from more traditionally regarded (physical) assets in that the more often it is used, the more valuable it can become, whereas the opposite is usually the case with traditional assets, which tend to lose in value and depreciate with use.

The value of information can be viewed from a range of perspectives; there is little doubt that it is a complex matter and one that provides many challenges to both the information and the accountancy professions.

Information can pass through a number of stages before it acquires any value. It may lie dormant, waiting for the right circumstance or application before anyone actually recognises and ascribes a value to it. It may be incomplete; it may have both a positive and negative effect; and a piece of information that is valuable to one individual or organisation may not have the same value for another individual or organisation.

Some organisations will see value in information that enables faster decision making, others will see higher value in information that enables them to be at the forefront of developing new and innovative products, and some will see higher value in the way information can be used to create competitive advantage. The old adage 'information is power' still holds sway in some professions. Each organisation is unique and its approach to attributing value to its information assets will depend on its circumstances. Value will depend upon aspects such quality, context, relevance, use and timeliness.

Quality

The quality of the information will be essential in terms of deciding how valuable (or otherwise) it is. No business can afford to work with poor-quality information; to do so would place it at a distinct disadvantage. Is the information up to date? Is it the latest available? Does the organisation archive 'old' information?

Linked with the quality of information is the question of integrity. Is the information unbiased? Is it objective? What was it original source? How reliable was the original source?

Context

The context in which information is used will have an impact on its value to the organisation. Information *per se* may not be of any great value, but when it is put into context and used for a particular purpose, it creates value for the organisation and becomes a prized commodity.

Relevance

Information will be valuable if it is relevant. The challenge in today's fast-moving business environment, where information is all pervasive, is to 'sort the wheat from the chaff' – to decide what is relevant and what is not relevant. Keys to success are being able to find, sort, analyse and exploit information relevant to the organisation's core business activities.

Use

Information becomes valuable when it is used – to make decisions, to decide on a particular course of action. Value is achieved through the effective use of information.

Timeliness

Is the right information available at the right time? Information that is received too late is of no value. Hindsight is a wonderful thing and many of us have been in positions where we have said 'if only I had known that before I embarked upon this course of action'.

The capabilities of information

We have said that information differs from the more traditional organisational assets; it is 'soft' and therefore more difficult to manage than 'hard' assets. Sometimes, when it comes to managing information, this is used as an avoidance tactic by organisations that feel challenged by its intangible nature. However, this should not be used as an excuse to ignore the important role information can and does play in helping an organisation to achieve success, nor as an excuse for failing to manage it effectively.

Some of the capabilities of information mean that it retains or increases in value in a way that would be contrary for other types of organisational assets.

Consider for a moment how large professional service firms operate. Clients employ them because they have a particular reputation and/or expertise gained over a period of time, and professional service firms often sell the same information, i.e., their problem-solving processes, to a variety of clients and generate fee income from doing so. In this example the same piece of information can be sold over and over again without losing any of its original value. Clients are paying for information and expect the firm to be able to present them with solutions to the issues they face. The standard solution may not quite fit the client's specific situation, in which case the client expects the firm to adapt and tailor the product (information) to make it work for them.

This example also demonstrates a number of other capabilities: the same information can be used and reused to generate additional value not only for the 'seller', but also for the 'buyer', who can in turn share that same information to resolve similar issues as they arise in the future. It is also quite possible that, by sharing specific information and using it in a similar organisational context, it will be adapted, refined, processed and used to create new information.

Information assets on the balance sheet

There have been and still are many debates about the financial value of information, and some commentators have striven to apply accounting methodology to the valuation of information assets. This has proved difficult, not least because the manner in which accounting standards have developed does not easily lend itself to valuing information assets. Physical asset valuations are subject to specific rules and treatments, established over many years, which cannot easily be applied to the valuation of intellectual assets such as information. Information assets are not usually subjected to the same level of analysis and control as physical assets, and their treatment within an organisation differs, sometimes quite significantly, from that of physical assets.

Trying to place a value on information is further complicated by the fact that it can be produced at very little or no cost; that a piece of information that is valuable to one individual may not be worth anything to another individual in the same organisation; that the same information can be used by many people at the same time, and that the constant use of information will not necessarily depreciate its value.

One might argue, of course, that an organisation could use accounting methodology as applied to other forms of intangible assets (brands, trademarks, goodwill, patents) to place a value on information, but this too has proved problematic; intangibles also have to be treated in a particular way and, once identified, have to be amortised over a period of time. We have already said that the value of information may well increase and not decrease over time, so to use this method may well produce a completely inaccurate valuation of information assets.

Somewhere between 30 per cent and 70 per cent of the market value of a company is accounted for by its intangible assets; this includes information. This picture is very different from that of the late 1980s, when the value of tangible assets more accurately reflected a company's worth. The fact that we do not have a consistent and widely accepted method for valuing information assets means that this very important driver of wealth is not being properly accounted for. If it is not being reported on, not subject to the stringencies applied to the management of other assets, there is a real risk that information will continue to 'play second fiddle' to other assets and consequently fail to receive the attention it rightly deserves, and fail also to be managed effectively.

There appears to be a growing consensus that accounting bodies should be developing a (new) method for the valuation of information assets. Until such a time, an organisation's information assets will remain off the balance sheet and not be given the recognition they deserve.

If organisations are required to identify and value information assets (for accounting purposes), this can only mean that information management as a formal discipline will be given more recognition and a higher profile.

Summary

In this chapter we have considered the importance of recognising information as an asset and why it should be given the same attention as other, more traditional assets, when it comes to managing organisational resources.

The Hawley Report, published in 1995, was instrumental in promoting the concept of 'information as an asset' and it sought to provide a framework to help organisations to identify the information assets they held and also provided a structure for the management of those assets.

The first step in the process requires an organisation to draw up an asset register; this can be a complex and time-consuming activity that almost inevitably will create debate about the value of information assets.

The value ascribed to information assets will depend on a number of different factors – quality, context, relevance, utilisation and timeliness. Each organisation will have its own view of the value of its information assets.

Some commentators have tried to apply accounting methodology to the valuation of information assets, but this has proved to be unworkable for a variety of reasons and there is a growing consensus that accountancy bodies should develop standards to enable organisations to be consistent in their valuation methods and to facilitate the appearance of information assets on the balance sheet. This would reflect a more accurate picture of an organisation's worth and give focus to information, which, after all, is a key driver of wealth creation in today's economy.

Toolkit activity

- Activity 5: Information as an asset

4

Information auditing

Introduction

In the previous chapter we discussed the idea of compiling an information asset register. A key tool to help identify information holdings (assets) is the information audit. It can be used to identify both internal and external information assets. The information audit can also serve many other purposes.

The audit can uncover how information assets are created, how they are maintained and how they are protected. It can be also used to identify information requirements and information gaps. The audit can also help in identifying information flows, processes and bottlenecks. It can highlight how information is used not only within the organisation but also with external stakeholders. The audit may also show up areas of duplication and (unnecessary) repetition, as well as any barriers to information access.

With the increasing emphasis on information compliance and corporate governance, an audit will also help to identify where legal and regulatory requirements are being adhered to.

An information audit can help to clarify the costs and benefits associated with information work and raise the profile of information as a strategic resource. The results of the audit can be a key tool in the formulation of an effective information strategy.

In an ideal world, the information audit will encompass all of the above, but it may be best to concentrate on specifics, particularly if the audit is being undertaken for the first time. The most important first step may be the creation of an information asset register, in which case the information audit can be performed with this particular aim in mind.

There is no doubt that an information audit can be both time and resource hungry, and in order for it to be successful it will need the cooperation of people throughout the organisation and should be championed by senior management. Be under no illusion that it is a significant undertaking, and a realistic stance is required if the right balance is to be struck between what is desirable and what is feasible, given the time and resources allocated to the exercise.

There is no universally agreed method for conducting an information audit. In some ways this is an advantage, because each organisation is different and has different requirements of its information resources; yet, on the other hand, the lack of a defined process can be a disadvantage because it can leave organisations struggling to define their own methodology for undertaking and completing the information audit.

If the information audit is going to be a successful exercise, the following will be critical success factors.

Make sure that there is a clear understanding of what the information audit is

A point worth mentioning is that the term 'audit' may have negative connotations within your organisation and participants (employees and external stakeholders alike) may feel that they are being investigated and scrutinised for errors and shortcomings in the way they go about their work. It may therefore be preferable to use other terms, such as 'information analysis', 'information review' or 'corporate information survey'. Be mindful of the language used in the organisation and use terms that are more acceptable (than 'audit') to the general workforce. That way you will win their greater support and cooperation and allay any fears and suspicions.

Make sure that you understand and clearly articulate the business drivers for the audit

If, for example, you are undertaking the audit in order to identify information assets, be clear as to why this is necessary and how it will improve operations; how it links in to organisational strategy; and the benefits that are expected to accrue from the information audit.

Be clear about the improvements the organisation wishes to achieve

If the audit is being undertaken, for example, as a means to identify how existing hard-copy information assets can be converted to electronic formats, promote the improvements that will result from faster and more efficient accessibility to key information resources.

Articulate the benefits the organisation wishes to achieve

Promote the strategic importance of good information management to overall business success. Remember that when anything new is introduced in an organisation, people will always want to know 'What's in it for me?', so make sure that you also address the benefits that will accrue to the employees.

Have clear objectives for the audit

Having clear objectives is crucial and will ensure that the time allocated to preparation and planning is time well spent. It will enable a purposeful approach and will help to ensure that all the activities undertaken within the remit of the audit are focused in the right areas.

Determine the scope of the audit

If you have established clear objectives, this should follow naturally. Think about who will be involved: one specific department, one geographical location, or the whole organisation? Will it focus on hard-copy information assets, electronic information assets, or both? Also consider what is going to be a realistic achievement within the timescale and budget available.

Use the most appropriate methodology for data collection

Prior to deciding on a methodology, think about the way in which the data you collect will be analysed. Will you be collecting a combination of qualitative and quantitative data? What analysis tools are available? You will probably be collecting data from a variety of sources, so you will need to think carefully about the best way to do this. We will touch on this later in this chapter.

Think about the best way or ways to communicate the outcomes, conclusions, recommendations and action points when the audit is completed

Typically, a report will be produced, usually in hard-copy format, sometimes in electronic format or maybe a combination. Should everyone receive a full and detailed report, or would it be better to provide a summary of the key points? Should the report be presented orally? Will it require some associated workshops? We will consider this and related issues later in this chapter.

By virtue of the fact that an audit is under way, you will get people to think carefully about the information assets they need and use and why information is such a key organisational resource. It will raise awareness of the need to give information the same attention as other assets and to manage it effectively, and will create consensus that responsibility for information, if this is not already the case, is vested at board or senior management level.

A structured approach is recommended, and actions will need to be taken sequentially. We will now consider the components of an audit, and present them in three phases – planning, conducting and reporting.

Phase 1: Planning an information audit

In the planning stage, consideration should be given to

- the audit objectives
- scoping and resourcing the audit
- methodology
- reporting.

Let us consider each of these in turn.

The audit objectives

First and foremost, you need to establish a link with the organisation's business objectives, and to do this you will need to understand its vision, mission and values.

The vision is a statement of what the organisation wants to be. It is the idea(s) that drive(s) the organisation long-term and will, ideally, be quite short and succinct. Vision statements are sometimes criticised for being too general, but the wording needs to remain applicable over the long-term and not require constant change. Once the long-term vision has been established, the mission statement follows, and this is the essence of the overall strategy: the organisation is setting out what it will do. Allied with the vision and mission are the organisation's values; a value statement will convey the behaviours expected in pursuit of achieving the vision and mission, and may also state how all stakeholders, internal and external, will be valued.

The information audit's objectives need to be linked to business objectives, otherwise it may just be seen as something that is adding to the daily burden of 'initiative overload'. Below you will find two examples of how an audit's objectives have been linked to business objectives.

In the first example, of an international financial services firm, the business objective is to increase market share within a specific geographic region by 3 per cent within two years (Table 4.1). In the second example, of a professional practice firm, the objective is to raise the firm's profile nationally by strengthening the different practice areas (Table 4.2).

In both instances employees can see how the audit will support and link in to business objectives. That way you stand a much greater chance of buy-in and cooperation, because it can be seen how the information audit will support the achievement of broader objectives and it will show how information can be used as a strategic resource.

You will also need to understand the organisational structure. Obtain a copy of the organisational chart, as this will help you to understand the relationship between different

Table 4.1 Linking audit objectives to business objectives in a financial services firm

Business objective	To increase market share by 3 per cent within 2 years
Audit aim	To establish an information resource database to support customer relationship management (CRM)
Audit objectives	To identify the information assets available relating to CRM: ■ creation, flow, use, management ■ value ■ impact. To identify information needed: ■ identify gaps and bottlenecks ■ identify duplications. To make recommendations for a sustainable CRM system.

Table 4.2 Linking audit objectives to business objectives in a professional services firm

Business objective	To raise the firm's profile nationally by strengthening practice areas: ■ attract new clients ■ attract quality staff ■ leverage information about practice areas ■ maximise the use of corporate information ■ improve cross-functional team working.
Audit aim	To evaluate, improve and promote existing information services and resources.
Audit objectives	To establish how well the existing services are meeting the needs of employees and the organisation. To make employees aware of the services and resources available to them.

departments and the flow of information between them, as well as identifying potential participants in the audit.

Additionally, you will need to understand the organisational culture. This will indicate whether information is regarded as a key resource and enable you to assess the value that the organisation places on information. It will also help you to ascertain whether you need to do any preliminary work to raise awareness, such as running some workshops to explain the information audit, why it is being undertaken and what the benefits will be.

Scoping and resourcing the audit

As mentioned already, undertaking an information audit is potentially quite a complex exercise and may involve many people.

Scope

The scope of your audit may be geographical. Will it cover the whole organisation or just specific business units? Will it focus on core business processes, such as HR, marketing, etc.? Will the audit be format based, that is, will you be looking at paper-based information or electronic information or at both? Will you be looking at internal information, at external information or at both? The scope of the audit will be dictated by its purpose.

Resourcing

At the planning stage you need to think carefully about the resources that will be available and what will be a realistic achievement, given any constraints such as time and budget. What resources will you need? These will include people, time, finance, physical resources and technical resources.

People

Who will be involved? Will an internal team or an external team or a combination of internal staff and external consultants perform the audit? Do you have the right expertise and skill-set in house?

The audit team needs to be made up of people who have different skills and expertise. First, the audit manager should be appointed. If this person is not a senior-level employee, they will need to receive the visible backing of senior management. Ideally, a team of people who have a mix of the following skills should support the audit manager:

- research
- data collection and analysis
- interviewing, facilitation
- IT literacy
- information management
- information literacy
- HR – staff development, training
- negotiation, communication.

Weigh up the pros and cons of using internal staff versus external consultants. Table 4.3 illustrates the advantages and disadvantages. The best combination may well be a mix of internal and external personnel. When using external consultants, be sure that you contract with consultants who have expertise in information auditing rather than in general management consultancy.

Time

There is little doubt, as previously mentioned, that the audit can be very time consuming. You need to assess carefully the timescales involved not just in planning, which will take up a significant portion of time, but in other phases such as data collection and analysis, which will require time and attention, as will the presentation of the final report.

| Table 4.3 | Advantages/disadvantages of using internal vs external audit team |

Internal staff	External consultants
Know the organisation	Lack knowledge of the organisation
Preconceptions	Objective
Reputation built up over time	Need to build trust quickly
Lack of skill in audit methodologies?	Skilled in audit methodologies
Adverse impact on day-to-day tasks/activities	Minimal disruption of day-to-day tasks/activities
Access to confidential and sensitive information	Denied access to confidential/ sensitive information
Participants give 'closed' responses	Participants more open
In for the long term; can see impact of change(s) over time	Short term; seldom see long-term results

Finance

The audit may be a costly undertaking. As well as direct costs you will need to consider indirect costs, such as staff time and the use of physical and technical resources. Establish the budget carefully and always think about building in an amount for contingencies.

Physical resources

What physical resources will be needed, particularly if you are going to bring in external consultants? Are suitable office space, furniture and equipment available? Will access to off-site document storage facilities and archives be needed?

Technical resources

The audit team will require access to office equipment, PCs, printers, scanners, telephones and photocopiers. E-mail and intranet access and also security clearance for external consultants may be required. Video and recording equipment will be needed if interviews are to be taped, and consider also whether you will need to employ any transcribers.

Methodology

How are you going to collect the data? Remember that you need to collect sufficient relevant information to be able to formulate reliable conclusions and recommendations. Choose a methodology that suits the organisation in terms of its structure and culture.

What types of research will you undertake? Will it be quantitative or qualitative? Quantitative data collection is numerically oriented, is collected from multiple respondents (all respondents are asked the same questions) and requires statistical analysis. Qualitative data collection finds out what people do and why, it does not necessarily have fixed questions and respondents may be individuals or groups.

In addition to the primary research (first-hand research conducted by the researcher) that you will be undertaking, will you also make use of secondary research (research that has already been undertaken by someone else)?

Always think first about how you are going to analyse the data before deciding on the methodology and do not be tempted to collect a lot of interesting but unusable or irrelevant data. Ideally, the data that you collect should be capable of being transferred into a database structure so that it can be analysed simply and efficiently. Software packages are available for analysing both quantitative and qualitative data. The former is much easier to analyse than the latter because of the open-ended nature of qualitative responses.

There are a variety of data collection methods; a typical approach will see a mix of methods being used. These are considered here.

Questionnaire/survey

When designing the questions to be asked, bear in mind the ultimate aims of the audit. Design and construction of questionnaires and surveys requires skill, and it is advisable first to do a pilot that will enable you to address any anomalies and clarify any areas of possible misunderstanding. Consider to whom the questionnaire/survey is to be distributed, how the data will be collected (manually or electronically) and what method(s) to use to communicate the request for completion. Here it is important to bear in mind what is the most successful form of communication within the organisation; is it via electronic methods, face to face, individual, group, newsletter, notice board, seminar? It may not be appropriate to use just one method of communication, but rather a mix of methods.

Interviews

You may want to back up the questionnaire/survey by doing interviews with a cross-section of managers and staff. Interviews may be structured, semi-structured or unstructured. The structured interview comprises the same questions being asked of all interviewees and the interviewer does not probe or question further. Semi-structured interviews are generally undertaken on the same broad themes with all interviewees, the interviewer probes and seeks clarification and can ask more questions. Unstructured interviews, while following a broad theme, are more akin to a free-form conversation. It is worth repeating that when deciding on what type of interview to conduct, you should always think about the way in which the data collected are to be analysed. Lack of structure can make analysis extremely time consuming.

Focus groups

These are usually formed to explore specific issues that have been thrown up by previous activities. Focus groups should not be too large, no more than say ten, as they can become difficult to manage. If you are to facilitate focus groups, then consider whether you need a separate notes taker, as it can be difficult both to be the facilitator and to take notes of what people have said. Alternatively, the focus group activity and discussions can be videoed and recorded to aid analysis.

Group discussions

Similar to focus groups, but the discussions may be general rather than specific. The same considerations apply.

Observation

Through walking around or spending some time in different parts of the organisation you can observe how information is used and how it flows in the organisation. Do bear in mind that normal behaviours may change when individuals know that they are being observed. Data collection via observation may also include looking at records and documents as well as supplementary data and statistics.

Reporting

At the planning stage it is appropriate to give thought to how the audit's findings, conclusions and recommendations will be reported. It is important to choose the best method, having given consideration to the structure and culture of the organisation. Options include a written report in either hard-copy or electronic format with graphics to illustrate data, and oral presentations.

Phase 2: Conducting an information audit

We know that conducting a first-time audit in an organisation will present challenges and that it will be a resource-hungry activity. As already mentioned, for an audit to be successful it needs the visible support of senior management, so before the start be sure that you do have such support. An audit should not be regarded as a one-off exercise, but rather as a process that is undertaken regularly (annually or bi-annually, depending upon how quickly the sector in which you operate changes). Second and subsequent audits can use data collected previously (if still relevant and appropriate), thereby reducing the time commitment required.

Data collection

What data will you collect and how will you collect it? How are you going to analyse it? These are all key questions that must be addressed at the outset. We have seen that various data collection methods can be used and we will now consider some relevant matters in a little more depth.

Questionnaire/survey

If you are using these (and they are the most commonly used method of collecting data in an information audit) be mindful of the following when constructing your questions.

The purpose of the questions

What information are you trying to ascertain? Think about the audit objectives. How is the audit linked to business objectives?

The type of questions – open/closed?

Open questions will present a variety of answers whereas closed questions are drafted in such a way that the respondent has to choose. Closed questions are less time consuming (for the respondent) and easier to analyse than open questions.

How many questions?

How long will the questionnaire be? How much time will a respondent need to dedicate to answering it?

When and where will it be completed?

Everyone is under pressure in a fast-moving environment; you may even face some hostility. So make it as easy as possible for respondents to complete; consider providing options such as online methods that allow participants to save existing answers if they have to break off in the middle of the exercise.

Layout of questions

Be consistent in your presentation. A clear layout makes it easier to comprehend and aids completion.

Order of questions

Make sure that the questions follow a logical sequence; group similar subjects together.

It is advisable to pilot the questionnaire/survey first, and that way you will be able to:

- gauge the length of time required for completion
- appreciate whether the scoring and rating methods are clear
- determine whether the questions flow in a logical sequence
- ask for suggestions as to topics that you may not have covered.

The pilot should include a relevant sample of the population already identified as participants in the full audit and it should involve key stakeholders.

When issuing questionnaires and surveys always provide guidance; clarify what information should be included and what excluded; clarify what is compulsory and what is optional; provide an estimate of the time it will take to complete; and always include contact details in case any queries arise.

Interviews

We have already outlined the different types of interviews that can be used: structured, semi-structured or unstructured. Try to build in as much consistency as possible, as this will enable easier comparison of results. Be aware of the need to offer confidentiality or anonymity and always be ethical in the way that you conduct interviews. People may be revealing sensitive information and must be able to trust that it will be used in the right way.

Try to limit the length of interviews to an hour at most and also consider the environment in which they are conducted. Do you need to be in a private area? Will they be conducted at workstations and, if so, what barriers might this create?

Interviews can provide you with very rich qualitative data, but will be time- and labour-intensive not only in the actuality but also in the analysis.

Focus groups/discussion groups

These are often used to supplement the data collected via questionnaires and surveys. A good approach is to distribute discussion topics in advance so that participants have some time to think about the issues beforehand. The most valuable data will come from respondents who feel that they are in a non-threatening environment and can speak openly about the issues.

Well-run group discussions can present a wide expression of different views; they enable points to be clarified immediately, are good for creative thinking, can tackle issues not raised in questionnaires and can be time efficient, as the views of a number of participants can be gathered in a single discussion.

On the downside, they can be difficult to set up; unless they are very well facilitated, they can lose focus and can at times be used as an opportunity to vent dissatisfactions between staff.

Observation

This can include key documents:

- mission statements
- business plans
- previous audits (if available)
- organisational structure charts (legal structure)
- job descriptions
- information strategy and policy documents
- information unit/centre tasks and responsibilities
- training programmes (information, records and document management and any information literacy programmes etc.).

Observation can also include supplementary data and statistics:

- number of 'hits' on intranet, internet, extranet sites
- usage levels of content management systems
- statistics from electronic documents – storage, use, deletions, amendments
- number and type of enquiries logged by information unit and/or library
- statistics on borrower activity from information unit and/or library
- statistics on use of externally provided information resources, e.g., subscription services, electronic journals.

Analysis

Once the audit has been conducted, the data you have collected will need analysis. If the data collection methods have been chosen with due consideration as to the method of analysis, then this should not be too onerous a task. Specialist research software tools can be used to analyse both quantitative and qualitative data. Alternatively, you may prefer to use in-house resources to assist with analysis, e.g., experts in spreadsheets or databases.

The analysis will provide you with valuable insights in terms of how information is viewed and used in the organisation. Depending on the stated objectives of the audit, the outcome of the analysis may include the following:

- an information assets register
- information types
- information processes
- organisational information needs
- organisational information flows

- information responsibilities
- information accessibility
- information bottlenecks
- value placed on information assets
- location of information assets
- compliance with legislative and regulatory information frameworks
- information good practices
- security of information
- IT systems.

The results of the analysis will lead to the formulation of recommendations and an action plan, which will need to be presented to the organisation. Good practice suggests that it is advisable to test the recommendations and proposed action plan with key stakeholders prior to finalising the audit report for wider publication. This will enable any misunderstandings to be addressed and will garner senior management support for the proposals in the final report.

Phase 3: Presenting the audit report

There are many ways in which the results of the audit can be presented to the organisation. The form and style of presentation will depend on the organisation and the context in which the audit was initiated. In the vast majority of instances a written audit report will be produced and its presentation in either hard-copy or electronic format may be supplemented by oral presentations.

The key to successful presentation lies in understanding the audience.

The audience

The audit report will need to be presented to the organisation and again, depending on the context, this may or may not involve presenting to the whole organisation. At a minimum, the report's audience should include the sponsor (senior manager), key stakeholders, management, participants in the audit and all staff affected by any proposed changes.

When writing the report, be concise. This is sometimes easier said than done, especially if it includes quite complex maps of information flows, so use charts and diagrams to illustrate points where appropriate. Make the report a working document with clear and practical recommendations and actions. Ensure that the aims and objectives of the audit have been met and show clearly the links to other business objectives and strategies. Always articulate the business benefits that will accrue from the action plan.

Structuring the report

The content should be grouped into major headings, with a logical order of presentation. You may wish to adopt the following pattern:

- Cover page
- Title page
- Contents page
- Executive summary
- Introduction/background
- Methodology
- Findings/discussion/analysis

- Conclusions
- Recommendations
- References
- Appendices
- Glossary
- Distribution

The sections should be arranged in a logical order. Main sections (1.0, 2.0, etc.), minor sections (1.1, 1.2, etc.) and sub-sections (1.1.1, 1.1.2, etc.) should all be numbered using a logical system and without over-complication. Illustrations, diagrams, graphs, charts and tables should be used where they add value to the commentary.

The main section headings are now explained.

Cover

A cover is not essential, although it is useful if the report is likely to be handled by a number of people. A distinctive cover can make a report easily identifiable.

Title page

This should indicate the subject of the report and include the name of the author, date of the report, and for whom the report is written. The title should be descriptive, concise and, above all, specific.

Contents page

The aim is to enable the reader to locate information quickly and easily. Main sections of the report, tables, figures and appendices should be listed, with the page number alongside.

Executive summary

The summary is vitally important and must be a brief account of the principal findings and recommendations. The aim is to enable the reader to see at a glance what the report says. It must catch the interest of the reader and provide sufficient information to give an overall impression of the content.

The executive summary should be written when you have completed the rest of the report.

Introduction/background

The aim of this section is to introduce the information audit, who instigated it and why. It can also be used to record the factors that prompted the audit.

Include an overview of the organisational mission and objectives and how the information audit links in with them. The aims and objectives of the audit should be included. This section should tell the reader why the report was written and comment on its scope and (any) limitations of the research.

Methodology

This describes the data-collection techniques used and should include any constraints or special methods employed. It should clarify why you chose the methods used and (if pertinent) why you chose not to use seemingly appropriate methods. Any possible shortcomings in the methodology should be explained. Include and justify sample sizes. Remember to respect any promises of confidentiality given to participants.

Findings/discussion/analysis

It is difficult to be prescriptive as to what this section will look like without knowing the precise details of the information audit undertaken.

Plan the presentation of findings carefully. This section must contain the facts, and the deductions flowing from them, in a logical order. Complex findings should be divided into sub-headings.

Do not simply present tables, charts, diagrams and graphics without summarising the key points. Place supporting data in appendices unless they are vital to the reader's understanding – do not force them to flick back and forth to find information. Additionally, do not assume that the reader will remember a point made earlier – if there is a link, make that link for them.

Conclusions

The conclusions are derived from the substance of the findings/discussion/analysis and should flow logically from the facts and arguments expressed.

This section provides the greatest freedom, but can be one of the hardest to write. Sometimes people have difficulty in distinguishing between conclusions and recommendations. A useful tip is to apply the 'so what?' technique to a statement: look at each statement and assess its relevance. Does it add anything to the argument? Does it support any of the facts already available? If it fails, amend or discard the statement.

Think critically. It may be appropriate to write the conclusions as a series of short statements. Group them in a logical pattern and sequence. They should be backed up by your findings and it may be useful to give the paragraph number(s) of the finding(s) that support a particular conclusion.

Recommendations

This is the most important part of the report, and the recommendations must flow naturally from the conclusions. They lead to a plan of action.

Specify what needs to be done, by whom and when. Detail short-term actions, long-term actions and, importantly, when the next information audit should be undertaken and lessons learned by the audit team.

References

If you have used other people's writings as sources (books, quotations, reports, articles) you should acknowledge these by citing the source in the text and providing an alphabetical listing of items in the references section of your report.

Appendices

These provide you an opportunity to include supplementary material and can contain information in narrative, diagram or tabular form to support the text.

Appendices should be clearly numbered and referred to in the main text. They may include:

- detailed inventories
- data analysis from software
- information maps/flow charts
- sample questionnaires
- interview schedules
- vision and mission statements
- key business objectives and strategic plans
- organisational structure charts
- job descriptions/specifications.

Glossary

If you are using any unfamiliar terms and expressions it is advisable to provide a glossary to aid the readers' understanding.

Distribution

For reports with a wide circulation it may be appropriate to include a distribution list to indicate who will be receiving a copy. You may also wish to indicate whether a particular recipient(s) is to view it for comment or for information only.

A good report should be readable, interesting, well presented and no longer than is necessary to convey the relevant information. Recipients of the report are likely to be very busy people, so remember to keep it concise and relevant and to use plain language.

The final report should be thoroughly checked and edited and the author must be satisfied with the content before arranging distribution.

Communication

Identify the most effective communication channels in the organisation and establish how best to use them when presenting the audit report. Be proactive and follow through on publication of the report. Hold meetings to discuss it and seek feedback on proposals. Channel senior management support to obtain organisation-wide buy-in for changes.

Think of the audit as a process and use the first one as a baseline. If it has focused on a specific area, refine it for use in wider areas.

There is a great deal to think about when conducting an audit, and one that has been planned well, conducted professionally and reported concisely will surely generate better outcomes than one that has not been given the right amount of attention at the outset.

Summary

In this chapter we have considered the information audit, which is a key tool for establishing what, how and why information is used in the organisation. It can be the basis for developing an information assets register and can also lay the foundation for effective information management policies and strategies.

Although there is no universally accepted approach to an information audit, this chapter has provided a practical, step-by-step guide to planning, conducting and reporting an information audit.

The audit, particularly if it is the first time that one has been undertaken, is a complex task requiring both time and resources. Senior-level sponsorship and careful planning are essential to success. If the required skills and expertise are not available in house, then it will be appropriate to consider using external consultants.

Toolkit activity

- Activity 6: Employing external consultants
- Activity 7: Questionnaire design

5

Information management in the organisation

Many organisations, if challenged, would own up to needing to 'manage our information better'; but knowing intuitively that there are benefits to be gained from implementing an information management programme is not, in itself, sufficient to secure the impetus and resources to do so.

The general perception is that it is easier to manage physical assets – land, capital, labour – than information, which is seen as 'softer' and the management of which is perhaps harder to justify in terms of impact on bottom-line profitability.

We readily refer to notions such as the 'information society' or the 'information economy' and many organisations consider themselves as 'information-intensive businesses', yet these concepts are meaningless unless they can be integrated with key organisational aspirations such as improving market share, reducing operating and delivery costs, providing innovative products, enhancing customer satisfaction levels and improving staff-retention rates.

To gain support and make the case for information management you need first, to understand the wider organisational agenda – the vision, mission and goals – and second, to show how information management supports and is aligned with broader organisational aspirations.

Each organisation is different and the way in which the rationale for adopting information management is established will, by definition, also differ. However, there are some useful pointers to bear in mind that may well help to build the case for information management.

The case for information management

One approach would be to take an overview of key organisational processes and ask 'Might they work better if the right information/right time/right place/right format model of practice were in place?' There are many examples of where a failure to adhere to this model has resulted in a significant and unnecessary cost to an organisation – not having all the relevant information for a tender document and missing the deadline; delays in reaching critical decisions, due to the absence of key information; poor record keeping, resulting in fines from regulatory bodies; duplication of work. And how many of us can recall the vast costs associated with tackling the 'millennium bug' because no one had kept a record of their original computer source code? There are many similar examples. Are there any in your organisation that could be used to help support the case for information management?

Another approach is to use the techniques so successfully adopted by business process engineering initiatives and analyse 'waste'. How does the organisation spend its time? It is estimated that approximately 35 per cent of time is spent on necessary and added-value work, the balance being spent on unnecessary activities such as reworking due to errors, duplication, time spent in meetings where nothing of any tangible value happens, and on activities that are no longer required but happen because 'it's always been done this way'. How do you spend your working day? One of the most powerful arguments for information management is that it could be used to significantly reduce costs by eliminating 'waste'.

Yet another approach might be to use examples of successes in other organisations that are directly attributable to information management. Examples include pharmaceutical companies earning millions of dollars from better management of information assets such as patents and licences; call centres that have improved customer service and reduced call times and costs by giving operators fast and ready access to information; information collected via store loyalty cards, enabling retailers to better target their goods and services to customers. These are just a few of the success stories of information being used to improve operations and bottom-line profitability.

Once you have established that information management has a role to play, assessed the role of information within the organisation and identified areas where you believe that a focus on information management could provide enhancement, you should be able to demonstrate the benefits to be gained and how neglecting to implement it could have a detrimental effect.

The critical factor here is that, in identifying information management opportunities, you have to demonstrate that you know the organisation and to show how information management can serve many organisational priorities. Do not invent priorities or issues in isolation; identify current areas of concern/focus and demonstrate how information management aligns with these priorities; show how information management can help to boost the likelihood of improvement agendas succeeding.

Some common misconceptions

In persuading the organisation that it needs information management you may find yourself having to address some of the commonly held misconceptions about information management.

Information management doesn't matter

Organisations fail to see how important information is and how and why it should be managed. If you find that your organisation is reluctant to embrace information management because it feels that it doesn't matter, then find some examples of where information overload has been the root cause of poor or ineffective decision making in the organisation. Highlight also the risks of failing to update information and thereby endorsing the use of outdated information.

Information is too 'soft' and cannot be managed

Information is seen as too intangible and too difficult to attach a value to. These notions can be dispelled if a structured approach to information management is undertaken by following the guidance provided in this book.

Information and communication technologies are a direct substitute for information management

This is perhaps the greatest misconception of all. Certainly, technologies have a major role to play in information management, but too great an emphasis on technologies has resulted in information management programmes failing to fulfil their potential. A large proportion of information management can be done without having to resort to expensive technologies.

Thankfully, awareness of the importance of information management is increasing all the time, not least because information, rather than physical assets, is driving the world economy. Consequently, the misconceptions about information management can be more easily dispelled.

Forming a business case for information management

To get support for an information management programme and the resources needed it is likely that you will have to write a business case. A business case is a reasoned argument that outlines the benefits (and risks) of the proposed information management initiative as against a 'do nothing' scenario. A clearly articulated and well-argued business case will help to convince senior management of the need for change and to secure the resources with which to make it a success.

Establishing a sound business case for information management may well be complex and challenging; however, if you are confident that initiating an information management programme can bring real, lasting and tangible benefits to the organisation as a whole, the process of formulating a business case will be a valuable exercise. An information management programme that has been built on a clearly established business case is much more likely to succeed than one without a solid foundation.

A business case provides a consistent message to many different audiences: information management has the potential to touch many aspects of organisational operations and the documented business case can also play a role in educating those who will be affected by information management activities. A business case helps to determine the strengths and weaknesses of a proposal; it needs to be thorough, objective and honest, particularly in calculating the costs associated with the project and any inherent risk factors.

Investment in information management programmes should be considered in the same way as any other new investments and go through similar approval processes. Do not shy away from this; if you do, what does that say about your confidence in the information management programme?

Who should be involved in writing the business case? If at all possible, consult people who have a good, overall understanding of information management – peers and senior management. Draw on their knowledge and experience and synthesise their views, opinions and plans into a cohesive document. The content will come from the range of people consulted, but keeping the number of writers of the business case to one or two people will ensure that the format and presentation remain consistent throughout.

Be very clear at the outset about what you are seeking support and resources for. Are you seeking permission to reallocate existing resources to do research into how information management can help to achieve organisational success? Are you seeking approval to establish an information management team to work on the initial stages of a programme; or for an information audit? Are you seeking funding to acquire new technology? Define clearly what you are requesting and, if appropriate, break it down into separate phases: it may be that a separate business case will be required for each phase.

There is no set format for a business case, so the structure of your document can be tailored to suit the proposal you are making. What you should ensure, however, is that it is clear and concise while providing the ultimate decision makers with sufficient information to evaluate your proposals fully and give their approval.

The following structure provides an idea for how you might approach the business case and some guidance as to the content of each section.

Executive summary

This is your opportunity to sell the information management project to key personnel in a succinct but convincing manner.

The executive summary should be no longer than two pages and should summarise the key points and recommendations. It should be written after the business case has been completed and should read as a stand-alone document. The executive summary should not contain any information that is not included in the main document.

Topics for inclusion in the executive summary are:

- description of the proposed information management project
- clarification as to why information management is necessary
- details of the benefits information management will bring to the organisation
- summary of the costs
- recommendations.

Background/current assessment/goals

This section provides an opportunity for you to outline the background of your project, where the organisation currently sits in relation to good information management practice, and the goals/objectives you hope to achieve. Keep in mind the broader business objectives and demonstrate how information management links in with and supports those aspirations.

A business case almost invariably puts forward short-, medium- and long-term goals. Clarify the linkages and dependencies between them; for example, a short-term goal might be the completion of an information audit and the longer-term goal associated with it might be to streamline activity to eliminate duplication of work within the organisation.

The project proposal

Be clear about what the project is, its scope and what it is to accomplish. Clarify also what is not within its scope. In this section you need also to state timeframes and the resources that will be needed for the project.

Cost/benefit analysis

Collaborate with appropriate personnel to establish what budget is available; do your research and speak to the budget holders. Involving them at an early stage will mean that when the business case is presented they will be familiar with the needed levels of expenditure.

Outline all the anticipated costs. You will need to justify the costs by identifying benefits. Can you identify potential revenue benefits from an information management programme? How and where will it save the organisation money? Can you quantify intangible benefits, such as freeing up resources and improving responsiveness to internal and external customers?

Providing financial metrics to senior management is absolutely vital because it enables them to make informed decisions. Unless you are able to demonstrate the project's viability by showing that the benefits outweigh the costs, then the likelihood of agreement will be compromised.

Risks

Consider any risks and how to manage them. Include proposals for a risk-mitigation strategy. One way of managing risk is to limit the scope of the project by selecting a pilot site where a few 'quick wins' can inspire confidence and demonstrate success. These smaller and shorter initiatives will help to build knowledge and assist you to move the project forward and follow it up with more extensive projects.

Options

Outline other options and the expected outcomes, including the 'do nothing' scenario. This shows that you have thought carefully about other options and why they are not so advantageous. You will be seen to be not simply putting forward your own case and promoting it without due consideration of the alternatives.

Implementation strategy

Include an action plan. Outline who will be responsible for what: the sponsor, the project team leader and the team members should all know what their high-level duties and tasks will be. You may also need to state why the person chosen for a particular role is the best fit and, if appropriate, how their (additional) activities may affect their existing responsibilities.

If external resources are required, the justification and the associated additional costs should be outlined.

This section should also include targets and milestones. Be sure to set out details of how success will be measured. Use both quantitative and qualitative methods of evaluation.

Critical assumptions

Explain the assumptions you have made and how they were arrived at. Clarify who was consulted and what, if anything, has been excluded (e.g., environmental factors, business processes).

Recommendations

Summarise the main points of the business case and make suggestions as to how to proceed with the information management project.

A business case is often likened to telling a story and needs to have a clearly defined beginning, middle and end. Incorporating all the facts and linking them in one document enables the reader to see the whole picture and the benefits the project will bring, both tangible and intangible.

Always bear the audience in mind. Make the business case interesting for them and avoid using jargon. Stick to the facts and present them in a meaningful way. Keep it clear and concise.

Writing the business case can give you a real sense of accomplishment, as well as providing a solid foundation for introducing an information management initiative.

Measuring success: developing performance indicators

No organisational activity can afford to place itself beyond the scope of meaningful review, and this applies equally to information management: if other areas of organisational activity are subjected to rigorous targets, metrics and measures, then information management should be no different.

The time and resources invested in a start-up information management programme are likely to be quite considerable. As a manager, you should be able to make some assessment of how the investment is working out. This suggests the need for some measurement of value to the organisation.

Metrics, often referred to as performance indicators or key performance indicators (KPIs), are the tools by which success can be measured. Metrics may be measured on a quantitative basis (i.e., numerically), for example, the number of hits on the intranet or the number of enquiries dealt with by an information centre; or they may be based on qualitative data, which is usually in the form of a narrative, that is, using success stories to demonstrate the impact of a particular initiative.

Establishing metrics for information management and monitoring performance against those metrics will serve a number of useful purposes.

Provide clear and tangible targets for the information management initiative

Metrics enable clear articulation of what is going to be done, by what time and by whom, and the benefits to be gained from implementation.

Establish success criteria

Metrics establish how success will be measured – this needs to be demonstrated in tangible ways.

Assess effectiveness

Metrics enable ongoing effectiveness and viability to be assessed and allow for prompt remedial actions to be taken if things are not proceeding according to plan.

Establish the return on investment (ROI) and internal rate of return (IRR)

Metrics will provide details of whether the investment in information management is really paying off in financial terms. Most organisations will want to see measurements based on the traditional ROI and IRR metrics.

Box 5.1   Working example of ROI and IRR

ROI is the difference between the cost of the investment in the information management programme and the anticipated measurable change, i.e., expected increasing revenues.

IRR is the difference between the cost of the investment in the information management programme and the anticipated measurable change, i.e., expected decrease in costs.

Let us consider a situation in a building company that tenders for large construction projects. The investment in information management using the right information/right time/right place/right format model will enable staff to create and submit more effective and timely tender documents, thus improving the rate of tender acceptance and thereby increasing revenue – this demonstrates the ROI.

Demonstrating IRR, the same investment may not have the effect of increasing revenue, but it may enable the tenders to be put together using fewer staff, thereby decreasing costs.

Information management is likely to pervade many, if not all, parts of an organisation; therefore using metrics to establish the impact is clearly very important. When you develop metrics (or KPIs) for information management, couch them in the terms that are used by the organisation's existing assessment and measurement processes. It is best to use familiar formats and to be consistent with other areas of organisational activity.

When developing information management metrics remember to keep them firmly aligned with business goals. For example, a business goal may be to improve customer response rates and to answer all enquiries satisfactorily within three working days. The related information management metric should not be something fuzzy, such as: 'Improve the dissemination of information to enquiry-handling staff', but something specific, linked, for example, to the quality of the information that the enquiry staff need to access so as to satisfy customer requests. You could therefore establish metrics that ask the enquiry staff to rank the relevance and quality of the information they are expected to use and set a target to 'increase the ranking from x to y' within a specific timeframe, such as six months.

When establishing metrics, always take care to ensure that they are focused on the right things, those things that will make a tangible difference and have a tangible benefit for the organisation. It is much better to have a few, well-defined key metrics in place that will enable a focus on the right areas, rather to have than too many metrics that may result in people being pulled in different directions simultaneously.

Try not to set up metrics that require a great amount of time to be spent on data collection; this may detract from the actual work. Collect only those data that are relevant to the goals and remember not to overlook the time needed for analysis and subsequent action planning. Automate data collection as much as possible.

Balanced scorecard approach

An increasingly popular approach to developing metrics in organisations is to use the Balanced Scorecard, developed by Kaplan and Norton, which links the organisation's vision, mission and strategy to measures in four areas (Kaplan and Norton, 1992):

- financial perspective
- customer perspective

- learning and growth perspective
- internal process perspective.

Because the Balanced Scorecard approach considers performance from a financial perspective and also allows an organisation to focus on non-financial factors it is particularly relevant in the field of information management, where so much value is created from intangibles.

If your organisation uses the Balanced Scorecard, then use the same process to develop metrics for information management. Figure 5.1 shows an example of the Balanced Scorecard framework adapted for developing information management metrics.

In order to ensure that activities remain focused in the right areas it is suggested that you have no more than four or five objectives (and related metrics) in each quadrant. As an example of information management-related objectives to include, some suggestions are provided below. However, as we have stated throughout, remember to make sure that any objectives are aligned with business goals.

Figure 5.1   Balanced Scorecard approach

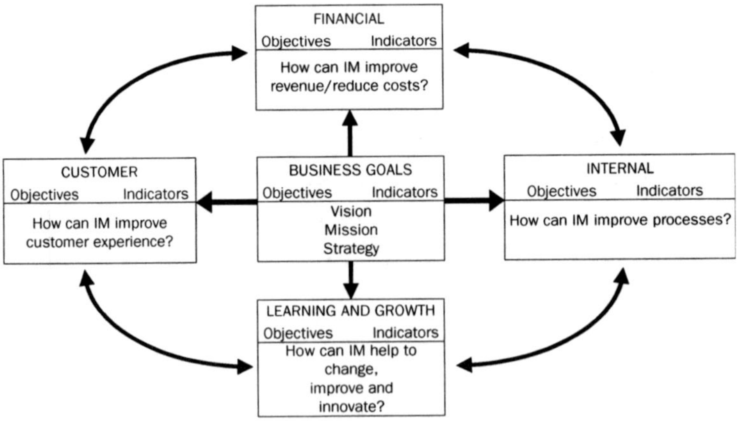

Source: Adapted from Kaplan and Norton (1992).

Box 5.2 Financial perspective

Operating expenditure savings

> Reduction in staff requirements (streamlining work, avoiding duplication)
>
> Reduction in duplication of subscriptions (journals, electronic information sources)

Capital expenditure savings

> Reduction in physical storage needs (due to digitisation of hard-copy records)
>
> Integration of software/hardware platforms for information management

Income generation

> Better management of intellectual capital – patents, licences, trademarks, copyrights

Savings due to reduced reworking

> 'Waste' analysis

Improved productivity

> Less time spent searching for business-critical information
>
> Reduced length of product development cycles

Efficiency savings

> Streamlining work activities through better use of information resources

Box 5.3 Customer perspective

Customer satisfaction

> Improved levels of satisfaction, particularly where advice/guidance/support is provided
>
> Call handling (time *and* quality)

Box 5.3   Customer perspective *(Cont'd)*

Accessibility of information

  Focus on intranets/extranets
  Navigation and searching
  Taxonomies

Improved cross-selling of products and services

  Improved conversion rate from sales leads, due to better information availability

Complaint handling

  Faster response time, due to better availability of relevant information

Service level agreements (SLAs)

  Using information to establish SLAs with customers

Box 5.4   Learning and growth perspective

Information literacy skills development

  Development of competencies via training programmes

Organisational memory

  Retention of information in organisation
  Initiating 'exit' interview processes, capturing information

Information sharing

  Culture change, team concept and team working

Staff morale and job satisfaction levels

  Improved by giving recognition to information sharing and team working

Staff recruitment and retention

  Information management activity used to attract and retain employees

Box 5.5   **Internal process perspective**

Information quality
    Information currency, relevance and availability
    Updating and archiving information
Standardising processes and procedures
    Availability of process manuals, training support, guidance
Good practice databases
    Standardised templates
    FAQs

Guidance on developing metrics

Once the objectives have been defined and agreed, the next step is to develop the associated metrics. How will performance be measured? The metrics should specify:

- what or who is being measured
- the target(s) to be reached
- the timeframe for achievement.

Where possible, it is advisable to establish a baseline so that a 'before and after' analysis can be performed. This will help to determine the success (or otherwise) of an initiative. An example would be to assess the number of average monthly visits to an electronic information resource and establish that as a baseline, and then to set a target to increase the average number of visits by a specified future date.

Metrics should be specific. For example, 'Promote information literacy throughout the organisation' might be too general. An example of a specific metric might be: 'Develop an information literacy training programme and run one workshop for each New Employee Induction Course'.

When deciding on a set of metrics always try to make sure that the relevant data can be obtained easily and that metrics can be measured accurately, consistently and efficiently. Don't set up metrics where the collation of related data becomes so time consuming that it deflects attention from the real work.

Re-evaluate metrics at regular intervals, at least at the twelve months' stage, and assess whether those in place are still relevant or whether they need to be refocused or replaced by new ones. Having a set of metrics that are in place for all time is not a wise approach, especially where the business environment is changing very rapidly. It is true that changing metrics will not allow you to make comparisons from one year to the next, but it is more important to ensure that you are focusing on and measuring the right things.

Key success factors

When presenting a case for information management in the organisation you need to be confident that, from the outset, you have articulated a view of information management that sets out the complex, long-term link between the management of information and organisational performance.

Demonstrating the potential positive impact of implementation, as against a 'do nothing' scenario, should enable you to present a powerful case for organisational buy-in from key individuals and to secure the resources needed to take matters forward. Support from top-level management is regarded as a key success factor in information management. Cultivate your 'champions' and use them to promote information management at every available opportunity.

Other factors found to be critical for success in information management are:

- understanding the organisation and its strategic goals
- provision of the needed resources – time, people, infrastructure
- having the organisational flexibility to cope with new ways of working
- integrated IT systems, which act as enablers of information management.

As with most new initiatives, individuals will want to know and see how their own roles will be affected, and this is something you must not dismiss lightly. Try to show the positive effects, particularly how people's jobs can be made easier and what success will mean for them.

Accept that information management will be subjected to the same rigorous performance indicators as any other organisational initiative, and embrace the need to develop information management metrics as a means to demonstrate its value and contribution to organisational success.

Summary

In this chapter we have explored how best to persuade an organisation that it needs information management and considered two principal approaches:

1 Taking an overview of activity and questioning whether the organisation might be more successful if information management were in place by using examples of where there have been failings or (costly) delays due to poor information management.

2 Alternatively, using examples of successes in organisations that are directly attributable to good information management. There are many case studies in the information management literature and speakers at information management-related conferences are always willing to share their success stories.

Building a business case for information management calls for careful thought and this chapter has outlined how you might go about making a convincing business case and securing the appropriate support to take matters forward. At a minimum, a business case should look at the effect of information management as compared to a 'do nothing' scenario. The 'do nothing' scenario will highlight the lost opportunities and demonstrate why this would be the wrong course to take.

Some information management initiatives have failed to fulfil their potential because they have taken an inappropriate approach, coupled with poor implementation and lack of metrics by which to prove success. Do not fall into this trap; develop performance indicators (metrics) that clearly show the value of information management and its contribution to organisational success. This chapter has stressed the importance of developing performance indicators that reflect those currently used by the organisation. An example using the Balanced Scorecard, which measures performance using financial and non-financial indicators, has been used, illustrating how it could be applied in information management metrics.

The chapter concluded with a look at some of the key success factors for information management. Securing senior-level support is of critical importance.

Toolkit activity

- Activity 8: The case for information management

6

Formulating information management policy and strategy

Introduction

The profile of information management policy and strategy formulation has risen since the mid 1990s, not least because of growing recognition of the importance of information and its management in a successful organisation.

Managing information strategically is vital to all types of organisations. Without effective management of this key resource, employees might easily improvise and manage information in disparate ways, leading to inefficiency, poor decision making, duplication of work, security breaches and a general lack of communication both internally and externally. Reputational risk and ultimately, in the severest of cases, complete failure of the business, could result from not having effective policies and strategies for managing organisational information.

Information management policy

What is information management policy? The word 'policy' comes from the Greek word 'politea' or citizenship, which implies that it belongs to all. An information management policy should therefore 'belong to all' the people in an organisation, and a carefully written information policy document will see information management placed at the heart of other organisational policies. Information management should not be an isolated activity; it should support the wider organisational policies such as finance, HR, marketing, operations, research, product development and any other elements of the organisation's activity. An information management policy will identify how information underpins all these other elements of the business and how it can be used to create success, realise competitive advantage and foster a cohesiveness that binds the employees together in achieving common organisational goals.

A policy provides a set of guidelines within which work processes are performed. An information policy, if effectively drawn up, will provide a set of guiding principles and will enable the organisation to recognise and appreciate the value of information and how it can be very effectively exploited to achieve the organisation's overall objectives. It will ensure that everyone knows the parameters and boundaries for effective management of information.

You should be careful that the policy refers to information in its broadest sense, structured and unstructured, and in electronic and hard-copy form. Do not fall into the trap that too many organisations have fallen into by focusing information management policies only on information systems and information technology. These are, of course, important elements of policy, but they are not the sole elements. If you focus only on these aspects there is a danger that your efforts to manage information will not be seen as critical to business success, and information management will not be seen as a key component of business and competitive excellence.

The information management policy will form the basis on which an information strategy is developed.

Information management strategy

What is information management strategy? An information management strategy should articulate how the policy is going to be put into effect, clearly stating what actions need to be performed. A strategic plan should be a tangible expression of measurable outcomes; it is critical to gaining acceptance at a senior level and you will need to demonstrate very clearly how the proposed strategies will add value to the organisation.

The business environment

The status quo of neither information policy nor strategy should be left unchallenged for longer than six months. In the fast-paced information society, policy and strategy makers must be critical thinkers and remain constantly alert to the changing business environment and the impact it may have on their organisation, and must ensure that their information policies and strategies are flexible enough to respond to any major changes, external as well as internal. National economic and political climates can create significant change within a relatively short period of time and globalisation means that international events now play a key role in how and where organisations choose to focus their activities.

As an example, consider the 'green agenda' and the impact it is having on the way businesses operate. We see major retailers committing to becoming carbon neutral within a specific period of time; service users being encouraged to accept bills for payment via e-mail rather than through the post; increasing pressure from environmental lobby groups for consumers to reduce the use of plastic bags, or for travellers to scale back on air travel. These are just a few examples of how the national and international agendas affect business operations. Will the 'green agenda' affect your organisation? What else is on the horizon that will affect your organisation? Do you have sufficient manoeuvrability to easily incorporate into your information policies and strategies any changes this will mean for your organisation?

We have already written about the importance of being strategically aware. The information professional with responsibility for information management must demonstrate an understanding of how the business works and how information affects the organisation. Establishing the strategic value of information, by means of appropriate policies and strategies, will ensure that you and the activities within your remit are seen as fundamental and central parts of the organisation. It will demonstrate to senior management how information touches all parts of the organisation and why (if this is not already the case) information should be elevated to a position where, without question, it is seen as a strategic and valued part of the organisation.

Developing information policies

The first step is developing the information management policy, and here it is important to explore and understand the organisation's vision, mission and corporate goals. Making sure that information management policies link in with these will set you on the road to gaining wide acceptance and recognition for the importance of information management in achieving the broader organisational aspirations.

Vision statement

Vision statements are forward looking and reflect where the organisation wants to be in three to five years' time, what the business will look like in the future and what the organisation's aspirations are.

Mission statement

Mission statements define the organisation's business, its objectives and how it plans to reach those objectives. Mission underpins and supports the vision.

In some organisations vision and mission are combined to provide a statement of the organisation's aspirations, values and goals. Sometimes the terms 'vision' and 'mission' are used interchangeably. Whatever the approach in your organisation, be sure that you have a good appreciation of the issues.

Corporate goals

It is important to ensure that the information policy is expressed in such a way that it shows how the management of information relates to corporate goals. Linkage with the achievement of corporate goals (the wider business strategy) cannot be emphasised too strongly.

Know your territory: what protocols currently exist for managing information flows across the organisation? An information audit will reveal the answers to this question. Informal arrangements and structures can be as important as formal, written expressions of intent. Think about how regulatory and compliance issues are handled, because this will provide an indication as to how stated information management issues are dealt with. Also consider how new regulatory issues are handled, communicated, introduced and implemented.

Find out whether there are any existing policy documents that refer to information in their title and/or content. This may provide some useful opportunities when you consider how best to develop information management policies. If you do find any such documents, determine what they say and who 'owns' them and make sure that the policy you are developing will not create any tension or confusion. You may well find that you can exploit such documents to your advantage. Also, find out whether any person or job descriptions, training or appraisal programmes refer to information management as something that is required of, or developed in, personnel at various operating levels. If such statements exist, do they have or have they had any practical effect? This may provide another useful lever for raising the profile of an information management policy.

The information audit (see Chapter 4) will also be key in developing an information management policy, because it will identify how information is being used, managed and shared across the organisation and will help you to see where improvements are needed. The information audit will be a fundamental building block in policy creation.

As an example, the information audit may have identified a large degree of 'silo working', resulting in information hoarding rather than sharing. You could then develop a policy statement that focused on information sharing and illustrate how better dissemination of information across the organisation would help to fulfil the vision, mission and goals.

Having demonstrated an understanding of the organisation's vision, mission and corporate goals, and after referring to the findings of the information audit, checking whether any existing policy documents refer to information and clarifying which individuals (if any) have responsibility for information management written into their job descriptions, you will be well placed to bring all this together and start developing an information management policy.

As with so many issues relating to information management, it is not possible to prescribe what your information management policy should reflect. However, Elizabeth Orna (Orna, 2004) provides some ideas as to what might be appropriate, starting with some basic obligations covering aspects such as:

- recognising that information resources are the property of the whole organisation and not the property of any individual or specific organisational groups
- every employee as part of their job should
  - be aware of the information they need to do their job as well as the information needed by the people they interact with
  - use information to keep their (job-related) knowledge up to date
  - share information and knowledge internally and with external stakeholders, to help achieve organisational goals
  - manage conscientiously the information they are personally responsible for
- the organisation has an obligation to provide education, training and support to enable employees to fulfil the foregoing obligations
- the organisation will respect that knowledge in the minds of employees is their personal property, in return for employees using that knowledge to support the work of the organisation and making it available to the organisation's knowledge base upon leaving.

Orna then outlines what might be included in an information policy:

- definition of what information the organisation needs to achieve its goals
- keeping the definition of information up to date

- undertaking regular information audits
- seeking information from external resources
- exploiting information to meet current and anticipated needs
- adhering to the right information, right place, right time and right format mantra
- identifying who is responsible for managing which information resources
- having a coordinated overview of information (and knowledge) resources
- promoting the sharing of information (and knowledge)
- developing and maintaining an appropriate technical infrastructure to support information management
- using information ethically
- accessibility and openness
- safeguarding information resources, past and current
- preserving organisational memory
- providing information management education and training
- developing and applying reliable methods of assessing the cost and value of information
- providing human and financial resources for information management
- using information to support change management
- using the policy to develop information strategy in support of business strategy.

To this list I would add the following:

- classification of information assets – ensuring that information is properly organised for use (by means of classification schemes and taxonomies) and having an agreed terminology or a common thesaurus

- requirements to ensure compliance with legal and regulatory frameworks
- establishing authorship and ownership, which will confirm who is the keeper of the information and who has responsibility for generating, maintaining, disseminating, archiving and deleting information in accordance with appropriate protocols and standards.

It is not suggested that *all* of these areas should be included in your information policy, but this does give an indication of some of the policy areas you may need to consider. The essential point is that the policy should avoid being too general; it needs to be clear and explicit, so that employees understand what is expected of them and there is no room for confusion. Ambiguous policies will lead to employees improvising and not necessarily acting in accordance with what was actually intended; such a scenario is a potential recipe for chaos.

Leading on policy development

The single most critical factor in achieving success in information policy (and strategy) development is that the identified leader should be someone within the organisation who has the mandate and authority to ask and to receive answers to the questions that this activity will raise, and should also be able to resolve any conflicts that may arise.

Policy development within organisations is usually undertaken at a senior level, often at board level, and many would argue that unless the board is involved it is failing in its duties towards the organisation. The Hawley Report was quite explicit when it stated:

> The board of directors is responsible for the assets of the organisation it governs and those assets owned by others to which it has rightful access; *information* is an *increasingly vital asset* in most organisations and is subject to changing risks and opportunities. It is an asset that is *less well understood* and less well handled than other recognised assets. (Hawley Committee, 1995 [emphasis in original])

Some boards may not feel confident in developing an information management policy and this is where the information manager (or equivalent) has a wonderful opportunity to provide support to the board of directors and, in the process, set out an agenda for good and effective management of information.

Some board members will delegate (and some may even abdicate) responsibility for information management policy formulation to those deemed to be the experts, and if they perceive that such expertise does not exist within the organisation they may seek external support from consultants. There is nothing wrong with bringing in and using external expertise to help with policy development, but ultimate responsibility must rest within the organisation.

What has worked well in a number of organisations has been to set up an Information Policy Development Steering Group. The steering group's terms of reference should include:

- overseeing and coordinating the formulation of an information policy to support the achievement of overall organisational objectives
- approving the information policy and reporting on it to the board of directors
- gaining organisation-wide acceptance of and commitment to the information policy

- determining and agreeing priorities for implementation of the policy, working closely with the HR department to ensure that sufficient and appropriate resources are made available for policy implementation

- using the information policy as a tool to set in motion the development of an information strategy.

Bringing together individuals from different parts of the organisation to form the steering group ensures that those who have a vested interest can have a full and frank debate about the issues. Policy development occurs in a critically constructive manner that takes into consideration the varying group interests and that results in a policy that stands on its own merits and clearly demonstrates the value of information to the organisation.

Gaining organisation-wide acceptance of and commitment to the policy

Once board approval has been obtained, the next challenge is to get organisation-wide acceptance of and commitment to the policy. Merely publishing a policy document as a stand-alone item will not deliver results. The information policy needs to be communicated, disseminated, supported and monitored. Try to be consistent in the presentation of policy, that is, use communications media and terminology that are familiar to employees. A good approach is to consider how other new initiatives, policies and strategies have been introduced to employees and to use similar tools and techniques to sell the information policy.

Gain cooperation by engaging employees in discussion about the implications of the information policy for their individual roles. Once people understand why and how they are expected to fulfil the policy, and its impact on them, the easier it will be to gain acceptance.

Some questions you may need to consider:

- Is board-level involvement required?

- Who will take the lead?

- Who are your champions?

- How will the policy be communicated? What fora/media should be used?

- What training and development activities need to be undertaken?

- Will additional coaching be required?

- How can information policy implementation be built into staff appraisal and development plans?

The policy should be clear, concise and realistic, and it should provide each employee with a framework on which they can build and develop skills to compete effectively in the information-led economy. In an ideal world, employees should be able to see how they can use information in relation to their particular area of work, where the linkages are with other aspects of organisational activity, and how they can develop their own information-sharing skills. By gaining acceptance for the information policy, you will be almost by default gaining commitment to implementing the information strategy – the actions that need to be taken to fulfil the policy.

Formulating information strategy

Using the information policy as a basis for information strategy development means turning the policies into objectives, targets, milestones and, importantly, specific actions. In essence, it you will break up a large undertaking (information policy) into a set of discrete and measurable actions. Information strategy development can be quite complex. However, if you have worked hard to develop a clear set of information policies you will have an excellent foundation on which to build.

Examine each element of the policy in turn and decide what actions are required in order to fulfil it. The challenge here is to recognise that strategy development is not necessarily a linear process and there may well be areas of policy that cross over each other. There will be variables, but you need to ensure that the strategies developed do not conflict with one another. The information strategy must be consistent and coordinated; if it is not, then you run a real risk that information management activities will compete for attention with other organisational strategies.

It is quite common for the information strategy to focus on a one-year horizon – good practice suggests that it should not be left unreviewed for any longer. It should articulate what needs to be done, by whom and by when. It really does focus minds on how the policy is going to be achieved.

As with policy development, strategy development will be more readily accepted if employees whose roles are closely aligned with organisational success are involved in its conception and development. That having been said, you do need to take a practical view and ensure that any strategy development group is of manageable size.

To illustrate what might be appropriate, an academic institution with which I work and which has a student population of approximately 16,000 and a complement of approximately 900 full- and part-time teaching and 700 administrative staff has an information strategy development group comprised of seven employees. The representatives reflect a range of roles. The members are the

Director of Information Services, the Deputy Academic Registrar, the Deputy Dean of the Business School, a head of school, a senior lecturer, a project director and the Head of the Management Information Unit.

Strategies must not be too rigid and should be flexible enough to allow actions to be adapted to meet changing circumstances. There is no magic formula for developing information strategy, but there are some guiding principles that may help you:

- the strategy should be a statement of a series of actions that articulates how the information policy is going to be achieved and by when
- it should contain milestones and targets against which achievement and success will be measured
- it should focus on key issues
- it should be realistic, practical and flexible
- it should support the information policy.

The information strategy can be expressed in many different ways, but for most organisations it is a written document. With that in mind, when writing it you need to put yourself in the shoes of the intended audience. It may be that different versions need to be written for different audiences. Always ensure that it is clear and unambiguous, that the content is in an easily understandable form (use diagrams, graphics, charts and tables if they add clarity to the text), that it flows logically and that it articulates very clearly how it supports the information policy.

To illustrate how the linkages between information policy and strategy might work in practice, the following case study – based on personal experience – shows how one aspect of information policy can lead to the development of specific information strategies.

Box 6.1 Case study

Organisational background

A training and development department based in a leading UK company had responsibility for designing and developing a training curriculum that reflected business needs. The training services provided to support the workforce (approx. 65,000 staff) included classroom-based face-to-face training courses, e-learning programmes, workshops, seminars, workbooks, coaching and mentoring programmes.

An information audit revealed that, in developing the course and programme content, the training department was responding reactively and only obtaining information (i.e., undertaking research) when approached by business units with specific training needs. It was not scanning the horizon to determine what factors might impact on the organisation; no thought was given as to how best to prepare staff so that the organisation remained competitive and at the forefront of its industry sector.

A subsequent benchmarking exercise revealed that the speed of development and quality of the training services was critical to competitive edge and that, if remedial action was not taken, the organisation would lose market share, its reputation might suffer and it would have difficulty attracting high-calibre employees.

Conclusions

Learning was regarded as being key to long-term competitive advantage; a leading-edge and strategically focused research unit was fundamental to the needs of a highly responsive training department.

Business objective

To create a world-class research and development function within the training department, focusing on key content areas and strongly linked to organisational business needs.

Box 6.1   Case study (*Cont'd*)

[Extensive international research was undertaken and the concept of 'Centres of Excellence' (R&D functions) was established as the way forward, focusing on key content areas (training needs) that had been identified by business units. These Centres of Excellence included Leadership and Management; Service and Sales; Operations; Systems Thinking; and Computing. They were tasked with providing access to the most up-to-date information in their specific content areas and ensuring that this was incorporated into the training programmes that were being developed and offered to the various business units.]

Information policy

To seek, obtain and exploit information from external resources to ensure that the content of all training programmes incorporates the latest thinking and ensures competitive edge.

Information strategy

To establish and maintain a network of external contacts internationally with business schools and universities, with professional and trade associations, governmental education departments and the UK Council for Industry and Higher Education from which the latest research (information) in the specific content area is obtained.

Research in the content areas to be undertaken using a variety of sources including the internet, libraries and relevant publications.

To ensure that learning and information (from the foregoing sources) is shared/made accessible to those responsible for the development of training programmes.

Monthly updates (via the intranet, newsletters) on the latest thinking and new developments in the specific content areas to be published by the Centre of Excellence Manager.

While this case study provides only a glimpse of how an information strategy was developed to underpin just one aspect of information policy, it nevertheless provides a practical example of how this might be done.

The information strategies were, in turn, incorporated into objectives within the performance appraisal process for each Centre of Excellence Manager and their reward and bonus packages were made contingent on the achievement of those objectives. Each one had to provide supporting evidence on how well the objectives had been achieved, comment upon what had helped or hindered achievement, and identify their own individual training and development needs. Reviews were performed on a quarterly basis.

As can be seen from this example, the strategy needs to be drilled down to an individual level, with specific responsibility for achievement being allocated to appropriate individuals. Always remember that it's the people rather than the organisation who implement strategy. Breaking down the policy into discrete, manageable actions is the key and allows everyone to see and appreciate the interdependencies between policy and strategy.

Implementing information strategy

After developing the information strategy, the next challenge is implementation. Many would argue that this is the hardest part and, to be realistic, full implementation may well take some time and is not something that will be achieved in the very short term. You may well have to negotiate a minefield of political and organisational obstacles before implementation is deemed to be successful.

Communication

The initial step toward successful implementation is to communicate the strategy. As with the communication of information policy, use the techniques that have been successful in the past when any organisational change has been proposed. By communicating the strategy you will be seeking to gain its acceptance and commitment to its execution. The initial response of many employees will centre on what it will mean for them and their role, as well as on trying to gain an understanding of the degree of commitment to new processes and procedures that will be required of them.

During the communication process make sure to use clear language and to avoid using jargon. Articulate the link between the information policy and the information strategy and make sure that this is clearly understood. Encourage open and honest debate; this shows that everyone's opinions are valued and helps to make employees feel part of the process rather than seeing the strategy as something that is being imposed on them.

In discussing the information strategy, present a scenario of the desired future state, that is, what the organisation will look like after implementation, and stress how effective management of information will help to achieve this. Show how it will translate into improvements for customers and other stakeholders, organisational team working and communication. Highlight the range of benefits that will be realised by implementing the strategy. Illustrate also the consequences of not changing.

It is important not to be too directional in communicating the strategy. Employee engagement is always easier if staff feel that they have contributed to the proposed changes. You could, for instance, draw on their involvement in and contribution to the findings of the information audit, the creation of the information policy and strategy development groups. These will all demonstrate how employees have been involved in the development of the strategy and help in gaining their commitment to its implementation.

Build consensus by presenting employees with opportunities and conditions for change. By adopting this approach you will encourage them to think about the changes they need to make personally in order to achieve the goals.

Resistance to change

There could be resistance to your strategic proposals, so you must be prepared to deal with comments such as 'It just won't work!' by demonstrating the benefits to be gained through implementation. People often regard change as a threat and staff may have concerns about perceived loss of power, autonomy and resources, about additional burdens on their time, about their capabilities, and so forth. Some will resist change as a matter of principle, so you will need to think through the issues that may be raised and the problems you may encounter. Plan how you might address concerns and what support you may need in this regard. In order to succeed the strategy will need people's commitment to change.

Winning key stakeholders' acceptance to change is crucial to gaining wider organisational acceptance. Identify your key stakeholders by completing a stakeholder analysis. This will help to identify not only your allies (champions) but also those who have the potential to wreck or disrupt implementation. It may not surprise you to find, on completing this analysis, that it is often the informal leaders who have a great deal of influence (see Toolkit activity 10).

Managing change and resistance to change are vital skills for information professionals and, indeed, for all managers. Change is a fact of modern business life; it is not new – organisations in whatever sector or industry are constantly subject to the vagaries of change. Reactions to change can often be predicted and managed; successful change agents understand the organisational culture and work hard to build consensus and support for new initiatives.

Organisational culture

After resistance to change, the next biggest barrier to implementing new working practices is organisational culture. E. H. Schein defined organisational culture as:

> the shared values, beliefs and practices of people in the organisation. It is reflected in the visible aspects of the organisation such as its mission statement and espoused values. However culture exists at a deeper level and is embedded in the way people act, what they expect of each other and how they make sense of each other's actions. Culture is rooted in the organisation's core values and assumptions; often these are not only unarticulated but also so taken for granted that they are hard to articulate and invisible to organisational members. (Schein, 1985)

When implementing information strategy you will need to consider very carefully the organisational culture and whether it is likely to be responsive to your proposals. Analysing and understanding the organisational culture will enable you to target your strategy and be successful with implementation.

The failure of many an organisational change programme has been attributed to a failure to understand the organisational culture. If the existing culture is not likely to be conducive to change, there is little doubt that you will have a significant challenge in gaining acceptance for and commitment to strategy implementation, and you may need to do a good deal of groundwork in preparing the organisation for strategy implementation.

Charles Handy identified four types of organisational culture – power culture, role culture, task culture and person culture (Handy, 1993). By identifying which one represents the type of culture in your organisation and focusing on the characteristics of that culture, you can gain a good understanding of where your attention needs to be directed so as to gain support.

Each type of culture is symbolised by a model.[1]

Power culture

The power culture is symbolised by a web (akin to a spider's web) of relationships.

The power culture is sometimes referred to as the club culture. In this type of organisational culture the primary influencer is the person residing, as does the spider, in the middle of the web. Power flows outwards from this individual, so the closer you are to the centre, the greater your own power and influence.

Often seen in smaller, entrepreneurial organisations where the original founder is at the centre of the organisation, the organisation's culture is driven very much

Figure 6.1 Illustration of the 'power' culture

by the style of the spider, who surrounds him/herself with like-minded people (hence the alternative reference to a club culture).

In order to get support for strategy implementation, you must first gain the support of the spider – the central figure.

Role culture

The role culture is symbolised by a Greek temple, the idea being that organisations are comprised of sets of roles/functions joined together in a logical, orderly fashion.

Organisations with a role culture are bureaucratic in nature and communication is very formalised; it flows upwards but very rarely across the organisation. The role culture is often seen in organisations that are long established. Stability, predictability and certainty are key and if any of the temple supports crumbles, so too will the organisation.

In order to gain support for strategy implementation, you need to get the support of each pillar of the temple, following the (formal) structures and protocols. This may well be difficult and quite time consuming. It is easier to achieve in organisations where the management structure looks both down and across the organisation.

Figure 6.2   Illustration of the 'role' culture

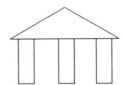

Figure 6.3 Illustration of the 'task' culture

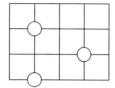

Task culture

The task culture is symbolised by a net, as power flows up, down and across the organisation in a matrix structure.

This type of culture is more flexible than a role culture. In a task culture people are brought together in groups, where skills and responsibilities are shared, to achieve tasks or projects or to problem solve. The groups can be changed or disbanded as tasks change – the cords of the net pull in different directions and allow for regrouping at will. This culture is often seen in consultancies, surgical teams, large construction projects and in advertising agencies.

Task cultures will often refer to 'coordinators' or 'team leaders', so to get support for strategy implementation you need to get the support of key decision makers and gain buy-in from group members.

Person culture

The person culture is symbolised by a cluster or constellation of stars. Here the stars, the individuals, are important.

Person cultures are seen in academic institutions and partnerships (e.g., law, accountancy, medicine). Expert or personal power dominates in this type of organisation and managers have very little control over stars (professionals). The stars attend to their own needs first and organisational needs second.

Figure 6.4   Illustration of the 'person' culture

To gain support for strategy implementation you need to obtain support from the stars in the constellation, i.e., everyone. This is the most challenging type of culture to work with. Increasingly, these types of organisation are recognising how difficult it is to rely on key individuals and there is a move, in some partnerships, towards a task culture.

Analysing your own organisation's culture will help you to understand whose support you need to obtain in order to implement your strategy successfully. Understanding and working with the organisational culture is a prerequisite for getting your information strategy implemented.

Training and development

If information strategy implementation is going to call for very different ways of working, you need to give thought to organisational competencies. You need to be sure that the people in the organisation have the skills and competencies needed to fulfil the strategy. A training needs analysis will identify whether there is a gap between what the organisation has and what it needs. Undertaking such an exercise will also enable you to see how and where training priorities should lie.

Tracking and reviewing performance

One of the reasons cited for failure of strategy implementations is the absence of performance assessment.

If the strategy is communicated and people are expected to implement it without its being reviewed at any stage, then it will be in danger of becoming just another document that gathers dust on the shelf.

For implementation to be successful, the strategy needs to be written in such a way that it highlights the short-, medium- and long-term objectives and how they will be measured. There is an old adage that says 'What gets measured, gets managed', so make sure that your strategy is couched in terms that include performance milestones and be clear as to how achievement will be measured. Initiate processes and procedures that will enable easy collection and analysis of data to assess how well the organisation is moving towards the strategic goals and objectives. Make regular appraisals, and review what is no longer necessary.

Also, clarify the linkages between performance and rewards. Compensation, promotion and special awards should be considered so as to recognise and acknowledge successful performance.

Strategic thinking

To implement information strategy successfully, you need to be a strategic thinker. You need to understand how to create information policies and strategies and be cognisant of the interdependencies between them. Never overlook the importance of ensuring that your information policies and strategies support the wider organisational goals and objectives.

Successfully implementing information management strategies is complex and time consuming. Information is an asset that is vital to success, and without robust information policies and strategies an organisation may struggle to compete effectively in its chosen marketplace.

Summary

In this chapter we have examined how best to approach the issues of developing and implementing information policy and strategy. There is a move in many organisations towards recognising the important role that effective information management plays in creating success and competitive excellence and, allied to this, the importance of having suitable information policies and strategies in place.

Information policies ensure that information is managed within appropriate guidelines and that there is a consistent approach to information throughout the organisation. Policies should encompass information in its broadest sense and not focus just on information technology and information systems.

Developing an information policy calls for a good understanding of the organisational vision, mission and wider objectives and goals. Information policies should not be developed in isolation, but must underpin the wider organisational objectives and goals.

This chapter has offered guidance on what to include in an information policy, and has highlighted the importance of board-level involvement and the need to secure organisation-wide commitment to the policy.

Information strategy articulates how the policy is going to be achieved and turns policies into objectives, targets, milestones and actions. Strategies need to be drilled down to an individual level, as it is the staff who will implement the strategy.

Strategy implementation can be difficult and is not necessarily something that will be achieved in the very short term. Be realistic in setting timescales for implementation activities. How the strategy is communicated initially will play a key role in securing organisation-wide acceptance.

You should be prepared to address any resistance to change that new ways of working will entail.

You will be more successful with implementation activity if you have a good understanding of organisational culture and how to work with it to achieve your aims. Identify key stakeholders and enlist their support at an early stage.

Consider training and development needs. Do not assume that people have the skills to be able to work in new ways without any guidance. Offer and provide suitable support.

Always remember the adage that 'What gets measured, gets managed', so track, monitor and measure activity and consider rewards and incentives for good performance. One of the most common reasons cited for strategy failure is the absence of ongoing monitoring of implementation.

Formulating and implementing information policy and strategy, if done well and effectively, can bring significant rewards and really place information management at the heart of the organisational agenda.

Toolkit activity

- Activity 9: Understanding your organisation
- Activity 10: Stakeholder analysis

Note

1. Drawings of models are used with permission of Management Pocketbooks Ltd.

7

Information literacy

Introduction

It is said that the amount of published information doubles in size approximately every eight years, so we are all constantly faced with the need to judge for ourselves what information is good, what is bad, what is relevant and what is trustworthy. In today's workplace reliance on information continues to grow apace and information literacy skills have never been in greater demand.

Paul Zurkowski, President of the Information Industry Association from 1969 to 1989, is credited with being the first to use the term 'information literacy'. In 1974 he described 'information literate' individuals as 'people trained in the application of information resources to their work'.

The American Library Association (ALA) defines information literacy as a set of abilities requiring individuals to 'recognise when information is needed and have the ability to locate, evaluate, and use effectively the needed information'.[1]

As an information professional you probably take information literacy for granted; you probably regard it as a natural part of the role you currently fulfil. However, colleagues in the workplace may not have well-developed information literacy skills to enable them to fully exploit the information they use on a daily basis.

In the UK, some business leaders have been openly critical in the press about the number of school leavers who do not possess basic literacy skills, not only hampering their employability but also having a detrimental effect on the country's competitive position. Emerging economies such as those of India and China, with their lower labour costs, are able to produce lower-priced goods than the developed countries and so the latter economies, unable to compete on cost, will be able to compete effectively in the global marketplace only if they have a highly skilled and information-literate workforce.

Information literacy has been promoted and well documented since the 1960s, especially in an academic context, in Australia and the USA. Its translation into the commercial environment has started and there is evidence of growing activity in this field, with conferences, seminars and programmes dedicated to the development of information literacy skills.

Information literacy is moving up the organisational agenda, and many of the reasons for this can be attributed to the rapid technological changes that have affected most organisations, leading to a proliferation of information resources. On a daily basis information comes to us from a wide range of sources, including the internet, TV, film and print media. Most of us would own up to having said that we often feel we are suffering from 'information overload'.

An information-literate person needs to develop a range of skills which include knowing when they need information, where to locate that information, how to evaluate it, and how to organise it, package it and present it. Information literacy skills, closely allied to the research skills of academia, also require an ability to read and think critically, as well as to problem-solve effectively.

In the workplace many of us are regarded as 'information and knowledge workers'; we are faced with having to research, to know, to communicate and implement a myriad of policies and strategies, as well as having to represent our organisations to external audiences. As employees we need to create, access, organise, use, evaluate, package and present information for a variety of purposes, often on a daily basis.

In academia, students and lecturers alike are required to read, process and analyse information from a range of scholarly texts, journals and books, the internet, lecture notes, conference proceedings and so forth.

Because of the growing complexity of our 'information environment' we are all faced with diverse and abundant information choices, in all walks of our lives. Increasingly, we receive information in unfiltered formats,[2] which raises questions about its authenticity, validity and reliability.

The availability of information through multiple media poses challenges for individuals in evaluating and understanding it. The expanding quantity and uncertain quality of information presents significant challenges for society as a whole: the sheer volume and abundance of information does not in itself create a more informed society. Individuals have to develop and use a range of information literacy skills in order to be able to distinguish the reliable from the unreliable, the relevant from the irrelevant. Only by being able to do this will a person be able to evaluate and use information effectively.

Information literacy skills provide people with the tools to assess, evaluate and understand the information choices they face; these skills are relevant not only now, but on a life-long basis. Some commentators make the linkage between life-long learning and information literacy and, indeed, many employers now expect employees to be life-long learners and in some professions (e.g., accountancy, law, medicine) there is a compulsory requirement for continued professional development.

Being information literate enables individuals to make informed, relevant and meaningful decisions in all situations, both inside and out of the workplace.

The workplace and information literacy

In the workplace information is a valued resource, and while job descriptions may not make specific reference to information literacy skills they are nonetheless highly valued and are an integral part of daily work activities for many employees.

Making intelligent use of information is the key to successful performance for many organisations, particularly those where information (and knowledge) management and use are key to achieving competitive advantage. There have been many studies of information literacy in the educational arena and it is increasingly being seen as essential in the workplace. Unless you are working in an information-led or information-intensive environment you may find that understanding both of what information literacy is and how the concept translates into actual practice are limited. Certainly, information professionals have an opportunity to raise their profiles by promoting the benefits to be gained by developing an information-literate workforce and the advantages information literacy brings to an organisation.

In terms of developing information literacy skills, many organisations have, understandably, channelled their efforts into developing a computer-literate workforce. Now the time has come to expand and build on the development of information technology skills by focusing training and development activities on the ability to evaluate information contained in both online and offline information repositories.

The volume and quality of information available to an employee continues to expand, as does the range of information delivery channels. These are becoming ever more sophisticated and complex, and so, to be effective in the increasingly multifaceted information environment, development of information literacy skills has never been more central to organisational success.

An information-literate worker is one who can:

- recognise when there is a need for information
- find information effectively and efficiently
- critically evaluate information
- manage and use information
- communicate and share information
- recognise the value of information.

Developing information literacy skills

As has already been said, today's working environment reflects a common situation in that we are all constantly trying to deal with an onslaught of information from a multitude of sources and in a variety of formats, to the extent that there are now real concerns about the increasing stress levels this is creating in the workplace and their effect on employees' mental health.

Information overload and the associated levels of stress are caused not solely by 'too much information', but also by not knowing how and where to find the information needed and, then, if and when it is located it, by not being able to understand it, not knowing whether it is accurate and reliable, or not knowing how to make best use of it.

Time pressures and the increasing requirement to meet targets can often mean that people are prepared to compromise by not evaluating the quality of information and not checking its source or authority. Failing to evaluate information effectively may mean that inappropriate or incorrect decisions are made, leading to potentially serious consequences for both the individual and the organisation.

Forward-thinking organisations are already developing information literacy programmes; they recognise the benefits of having an information-literate workforce – employees are more effective, can cope with the ambiguity and complexity of working in a fast-changing global environment and are not daunted by having to work with uncertain and unstructured information.

A key aspect of becoming information literate is that an individual recognises the importance of not taking information at face value and is able to use some effective techniques to assess and evaluate information for quality and reliability.

Information is an important resource and not one that can be ignored. There is no one perfect way of developing information literacy skills, but some useful tips and techniques can be employed to develop competence in this area.

The internet and information literacy

The internet is often the first place where people go to seek information. It is an important information resource and growing exponentially, with new sites becoming available at an increasing rate. With the advent of wireless technology, accessibility is growing all the time and no other medium provides so much information, literally at the touch of a button.

However, the internet is unregulated and some of the information it gives access to is inaccurate, out of date and really not very reliable. Sometimes the way that information is presented looks extremely professional and, in the absence of information literacy skills, one could easily be taken in by a stylish presentation. There is a risk in thinking that if it looks good, it must be good. An information-literate person will look beyond the presentation and use proven tools and techniques to evaluate the information and assess its reliability.

Let's remind ourselves of some basic facts about the internet.

All websites have an address known as the Uniform Resource Locator (URL), which indicates where information is located on the World Wide Web. If you know the URL of the website you wish to access, all you need do is key it in to the browser. The browser is a software application used to find and display web pages. The two most popular browsers are Microsoft Internet Explorer and Mozilla Firefox.

The following explains the components of a URL, using the BBC website, http://www.bbc.co.uk, as an example:

- **http** defines which Internet Protocol (IP) to use. If you are typing in a World Wide Web (www) site, you normally do not have to type 'http' because browsers use it by default.

  Sometimes you will see that the IP is 'https'. The additional 's' indicates a secure site: these are mainly used for financial transactions, e.g., online credit card payments and online banking.

- **www** indicates that the page is found on the World Wide Web.

  The terms 'internet' and 'www' are often used interchangeably, but they are not in fact the same thing. The internet is an international system of computer networks where a user of one computer can link in and obtain information from other computers. The internet is made up of a number of different applications, one of which is the World Wide Web. Other applications include File Transfer Protocol (FTP), newsgroups, e-mail and chatrooms.

- **www.bbc.co.uk** indicates the home page of the BBC website.

  Further detail in the URL indicates a specific document or page on the website. For example, the URL to go directly to a BBC radio station, Radio 4 is http://www.bbc .co.uk/radio4 and you can drill down further to a specific programme, such as the *Today* programme, by keying in http://www.bbc.co.uk/radio4/today, and even further to a specific item featured in the programme.

- The **.co** extension indicates the type of website – in this case a commercial website.

- The **.uk** extension indicates the country in which the domain (the name of the website) is registered (US domains usually operate without a country designation). All domain names have to be registered with a naming authority.

The extensions listed in Table 7.1 are those most commonly seen in URLs.

Evaluating online information

Having accessed the website what do you need to look for to satisfy yourself that the information it provides is reliable?

Initially, think about the meaning of the extension. For example, .gov is only available to government departments, so you can be sure where the information on a .gov website is coming from. Similarly, military authorities only use

Table 7.1   Common extensions for URLs

Extension	Meaning	Restrictions
.ac	Academic institutions e.g. universities	Restricted to academic institutions
.biz	Small business	Unrestricted
.com or .co	Commercial	Unrestricted
.edu	Educational institutions e.g. schools, colleges (and universities in the US)	Restricted to educational institutions
.gov	Government departments	Restricted to government
.info	Resource sites	Unrestricted
.mod	Ministry of Defence (UK)	Restricted to MoD
.mil	Military (US)	Restricted to the Military
.net	Network – commonly used by Internet Service Providers, web-hosting sites and others involved with the internet's infrastructure. Some businesses use .net for their intranet sites	Unrestricted
.org	Non-commercial organizations, e.g. charities, trade bodies, professional associations	Unrestricted (previously it was restricted)
.tv	Multi-media sites; used by the entertainment industry	Unrestricted. The California company dotTV is the exclusive registry for .tv domain names.
.uk, .ca, .ru, etc.	Country code e.g. UK, Canada, Russia, etc.	Restricted to the country in which the domain is registered

.mil or .mod, schools, colleges and universities use .edu or .ac, so these also give an indication as to the reliability of a website's content. The most popular extension is .com, which is unrestricted and so can be used by anyone.

By considering what the extension means, you may be able to tell immediately what the purpose of the website is (Table 7.2). Is it a commercial site, an information site or one that is seeking to influence and persuade you of a particular viewpoint? Can you tell the difference?

Once you have identified a relevant website/source of online information there are many aspects to consider. They

Table 7.2 Purpose of websites

Type	Purpose	Owner	Comments
Commercial	To sell products and services	Commercial organisations, businesses wishing to build a national and/or international presence on the internet	Commercial sites will typically provide information about their owner's sphere of operations, products and services. If you use information from a commercial site it may be biased, so you may need to look elsewhere to obtain a balanced or objective view.
Informational	Provision of access to information and other resources	Educational institutions, government departments, publishers, professional associations, individuals	These sites are not usually promoting a specific point of view so they are likely to be more balanced, but you should still exercise caution.
Influencing	To garner support for particular opinions	Individuals, campaigning organisations	It is important to understand and appreciate the purpose of such sites (including blogs), which are trying to persuade you to a particular point of view. There may not be any counter-argument presented, so the information could be extremely biased.

are presented and considered here under five headings: accuracy, authority, objectivity, currency and coverage.

Accuracy

Does the site contain obvious errors and omissions? Is there evidence of quality control? Does the website owner employ editors and fact checkers? Is it regularly updated to incorporate the latest information? Does the site provide diverse perspectives on a topic or does it promote a single view? Are information sources clearly cited?

Remember that anyone can publish on the web and that there are no standards to ensure the accuracy of published information.

Authority

What are the author's credentials and qualifications for writing on the particular subject? Knowing their educational or occupational background can help to determine the reliability and authority of the work. It can, however, be difficult to establish the authorship of web resources – even if an author's name is published, their qualifications/ experience may not always be provided.

Do authors clarify their purpose and content? Do they acknowledge their sources and provide citations?

Do they provide contact details? Are they willing to accept feedback, comments and questions?

Is the author an organisation rather than a person? If the author is not named, then consider the reputation of that organisation. Is the article one that has been peer reviewed?

How reputable is the publisher? Are you viewing information from a personal home page, from a site affiliated to an educational body or from a well-regarded institution?

Objectivity

Is the information presented objectively and without bias? Is any bias explicit or hidden? Does any bias affect the usability of the information? Is there advertising on the page, and to what extent might this influence the viewpoint? To what extent is the information trying to sway the opinion of the reader?

The web often functions as a virtual soapbox, so anyone can voice their opinions; the goals/aims of persons or groups presenting material are not always clearly stated.

Currency

Is the content of the work up to date? Is the information current enough for your purposes? Is the publication date clearly indicated? If not, is there a way to determine the date? Publication dates are not always included on web pages; if they are, they can have different meanings, such as date first created, date published on the web, date last revised.

Do any links work properly and lead you to active sites?

Coverage

How well does the site cover the subject matter? What topics are included in the work? To what depth are topics explored? Have you looked at sites with similar information, and do they include more information or opposing viewpoints?

Web coverage may differ from print or other media coverage; often the coverage of a topic is greatly influenced by the specific audience for which it was written.

Documents on the web sometimes include 'read me' or 'about this' sections from which it is possible to gauge the likely coverage. However, in reality it is often hard to determine the extent of web coverage.

Print media and information literacy

Print media are easier to evaluate for reliability than online sources because, prior to publication, they usually go through an editorial process that provides some comfort as to accuracy and reliability. Different types of publication are subjected to different levels of review and fact checking. Some publications, such as peer-reviewed scholarly journal articles, are reviewed 'blind' by an editorial committee and have to meet stringent criteria before being accepted for publication.

Many publishers of print media have their own editorial and publication standards, with which a writer has to comply before the work is deemed suitable for publication. Acting as a filter, these standards provide some assurance as to reliability, but a reader must still take responsibility for evaluating information found in print media.

In a similar way to evaluating online information, there are useful guidelines that can assist in evaluating print media, and the questions that should be explored are considered here.

Author

What are the author's credentials? What authority do they have on the subject matter? Do they have a reputation in the field? Are they known for their expertise on the subject matter? Have you seen the author's name cited in other sources of information? Does the author have an association with a reputable institute, organisation or government department?

Information about the author is often contained in books and articles – this is useful in that it gives you background information to help you establish their credentials.

Affliation

Whom does the author work for or represent? Are they representing the views of that organisation (e.g., a research group, a campaigning group, a policy group) or is this their own personal opinion? Look for disclaimers. What do you know about the organisation? How credible would they be to your target audience?

Think about possible subject or political bias. If an author is writing about the safety of genetically modified foods and has an affiliation to a large agro-chemical business this may cause you to question any bias in the published work.

Publication date

When was the information published? Is it current or out of date for your topic? Some topics are in areas that change rapidly (sciences), whereas material in other areas does not date so quickly (humanities). If you are dealing with government policy you will need to keep abreast of proposed policy changes to ensure that you are working with the latest information. This is particularly relevant if there has been a change of government or if new policy initiatives have been proposed in election manifestos.

Edition or revision

Is the information source the first edition? Later editions indicate that the information has been revised and updated to reflect changes in knowledge. If a source has been printed many times, this may indicate that the work has become a standard source in the area and is very reliable.

Publisher

Take note of the publisher. If, for example, it is a university press, then the work is likely to be scholarly/academic and aimed at such an audience.

While a publisher may be regarded as reputable this does not necessarily guarantee quality; however, it does indicate that the publisher may have a high regard for the author.

Journals

Is the article published in a refereed scholarly journal, a business journal or a popular title? The distinction is important because it will indicate different levels of complexity in conveying ideas.

A refereed scholarly journal is one that is published for 'experts', and before an article is accepted for publication it has to go through a peer-review process – a group of acknowledged experts in the field review the content for its soundness and academic value. Refereed sources will almost always include bibliographic citations and these can be used to evaluate the breadth and depth of prior reading and to authenticate what has been written, as well as being useful sources of further information.

Business titles concentrate on a particular field of interest. Typically, people – not necessarily trained journalists – who have an interest in the subject matter write the articles. These articles do not go through a peer-review process. They may contain bibliographic citations.

Popular magazines will include general interest magazines such as *The Economist* (UK) and *Time* (US) and tend to be written by staff writers or freelance journalists – the articles are geared towards a general audience and will be shorter than those in refereed or business journals. They are unlikely to contain bibliographic citations.

Having considered the above, turn your attention to the content and evaluate that. Again, there are some useful tips that you can use to assist you.

Print media content analysis

Audience

What type of audience has the material been written for? Is it aimed at a specialised or a general audience? Is it aimed at an internal or external audience? Is the information simple, technical, advanced or appropriate for your needs?

Reasoning

Does the information contain facts, opinions or propaganda? It is not always easy to separate fact from opinion. Facts can usually be established; opinions, though they may be based on facts, stem from the way that those facts have been interpreted. Articulate and experienced writers can make you think that their interpretations are, indeed, facts.

Does the information appear to be valid and well researched – is it supported by evidence? Is it questionable and unsupported by evidence? Have reasonable assumptions been made? Are there any obvious errors or omissions?

Are the ideas and arguments advanced similar to those in other works you have read on the same topic? If an author departs radically from and challenges the views of others in the same field, you need to take additional care in examining their ideas. That is not to say that they are incorrect in their particular views: they may in fact be presenting a new theory based on sound research.

Is the author's point of view impartial and objective? Is the language used free of emotive words and bias?

Coverage

Does the information you have gathered update other sources and/or substantiate other material you have read? Does it provide new information and/or new ideas? Does it cover your topic fully or only make reference to it? You should gather enough information to explore a variety of viewpoints.

Does the evidence used to support the argument(s) emanate from primary or secondary sources? Has the author conducted their own (primary) research to support their hypothesis or are they relying on secondary sources, e.g., research undertaken by others, or other published literature?

Style of writing

Is the material written and organised in a logical flow? Are the principal points clearly presented? Do you find the writing style easy to read or not? Be careful not to dismiss the content just because you find it a difficult read. Does the author keep repeating their argument? Are the same points made over and over again?

Evaluative reviews

When using books, in particular, seek out any reviews that may have been written – journals are a good source of book reviews. Are the reviews positive? Is the work considered to be a valuable contribution to the body of literature in the field? Do the reviews mention other books and might these be worth exploring? Is there consistency between various reviewers or has the material aroused any controversy?

Information literacy: further aspects to consider

You may also need to consider other aspects when assessing/evaluating information.

Political and economic interests

How might political and economic interests prevent publication of the whole truth? Has the material been aimed at a particular audience? Has it been published by a political 'think tank' and, if so, what is its leaning – left or right wing?

Think about how easy or difficult it might be for others to publish an alternative view. Freedom of speech is taken for granted in many countries, but there are countries where people can be punished or even imprisoned for expressing a view different from 'the party line'.

Numbers and statistics

It is important to check any numerical data and be wary of authors who use words to imply such data. Are the words 'most' and/or 'many' used to convey a point of view, e.g., *most* people said that they preferred beach holidays to walking holidays? 'Most' is very vague and you would need to explore in more depth, asking questions such as 'How many people were asked?', 'How many preferred beach holidays?', 'Under what circumstances did they express their preferences?'

Notice when percentages are given to demonstrate a point. A statement that 60 per cent preferred beach holidays and 40 per cent preferred walking holidays appears convincing, but is the difference significant? If 1,000 people were asked and 600 preferred beach holidays this might be persuasive. But if 10 people were asked and 6 preferred beach holidays, this would be a less persuasive 60 per cent. Be aware that percentages can be used to make insufficient data look impressive.

As to sample sizes, a very small increase in the sample size can have a significant impact on an earlier result and completely overturn it. In the example above, if two more people are asked, taking the sample size to 12, and both prefer walking holidays, there will be 6 for each preference, making the percentage 50 for each. Between 300 and 1,000 participants is generally regarded as a reasonable sample for statistics to be considered significant.

A sample should be representative of the overall population or group: if all the people questioned about holidays are employees of travel companies, the sample may not be considered representative. Similarly, if only teenagers are asked, it will not be safe to generalise from them to the rest of the population. To make a sample representative, a researcher should include a mix of people from different ages and backgrounds.

Data collection

In the above example, if you knew that those who said they preferred beach holidays had been entered into a prize draw, you might wonder whether they had an ulterior motive in stating their preference, which would lead you to question the reliability of the data.

It is important to ascertain the conditions under which data have been collected, so as to determine how much reliance should be placed on them. Research-based articles in scholarly and academic journals will normally provide full details about the conditions of data collection. They will also state any limitations of the data collection methods. Look for a heading 'Methodology' in the work.

Language

A clever writer can use language that is emotive or persuasive so as to elicit a position of trust in the reader. For example, if you read an article based on an 'experiment' does this suggest to you that some detailed work has been undertaken and that it is scientifically accurate and reliable? This may not be the case – an experimental approach may have been taken but this is not a guarantee of accuracy.

Emotive words and phrases such as 'unfair', 'unique', 'devastating loss', 'radical thoughts', 'poverty stricken', can create an emotional response that may lead the reader to a particular view and away from an objective and accurate appraisal of the content. Emotive words that are further backed up by emotive images (starving children, mourners at a funeral service, mistreated animals) can be quite powerful in channelling the reader's thoughts in a particular direction.

Persuasive language can influence you to form a particular view – words such as 'undoubtedly', 'unmistakably', 'surely'. They may be evident, but you still need to be alert to the use of a persuasive tone. Is the persuasive language supported by evidence? If not, then proceed with due caution.

Summary

In this chapter we have considered information literacy and why the development of information literacy skills, a common requirement in the educational environment, is emerging as an important issue in the workplace. Although job descriptions and competency profiles may not specifically refer to information literacy, it is highly valued and there is a growing appreciation of the benefits it brings to today's information-intensive workplace.

There is no one way of developing information literacy skills and one organisation's requirements will differ from those of another, depending on the level and extent of information-led activities. However, there are useful techniques to help develop the requisite skills.

This chapter has sought to highlight some fundamental points, particularly in the evaluation of online and offline information sources.

Today's increasingly sophisticated information environment places many demands on employees. Information is available in a multitude of formats and through a range of channels; its reliability is often questionable, so there has never been a greater demand for organisations to think seriously about focusing their efforts on developing an information-literate workforce.

Toolkit activity

■ Activity 11: Developing information literacy skills

Notes

1. ALA, 1989, www.ala.org/ala/acrl/acrlpubs/whitepapers/presidential.cfm.
2. Examples include information from biased internet search engines, e.g., search engines that may report results based on popularity rather than on relevance of information, or that may be subject to domestic political pressures; SPAM; and data that has not been analysed.

8

Information management compliance

Introduction

Information management compliance is increasingly becoming a key agenda item for organisations in both the public and private sectors. An increasing number of industry standards, legislation and internal initiatives is being passed that require organisations to ensure that information management activities are undertaken in line with appropriate rules and regulations. All organisations, regardless of size, are affected and failure to manage information within the applicable frameworks can have serious and far-reaching consequences. High-profile corporate collapses (such as Enron and WorldCom in the US, Parmalat in Italy) have demonstrated, very sharply, how failure to manage information in accordance with prescribed procedures can have an adverse effect.

Long before the eventual collapse of Arthur Andersen, the accountancy firm associated with Enron, clients had started to take their business elsewhere because they were beginning to lose faith in Andersen's ability to manage its information effectively. In the UK, a leading software company suspended its founder after accounting irregularities were discovered. The company's share price fell by 75 per cent as the irregularities came to light and affected (reported) future profitability.

The market value of a US-based pharmaceutical company fell by $30bn when the public learned that research into one of its drugs, which questioned its safety, had been delayed and not been placed in the public domain.

Misunderstandings on the part of the police as to the requirements of the UK Data Protection Act led to a situation where information about an individual who had been the subject of criminal investigations was not passed on and, as a consequence, that person became employed as a school caretaker and subsequently murdered two pupils (the 2002 'Soham murders' case).

There have been instances of corporate fines and, indeed, prison sentences being imposed on individuals who have failed to comply with the required legislation. An added concern is that even though mismanagement of information and failure to comply with regulations may not have been deliberate, this is not a valid defence. One of the largest fines imposed by a court (in the USA in 2004) related to a situation where information (evidence) had been unintentionally destroyed.

These cases and other similar instances have forced organisations to reassess their own procedures for information creation, access, distribution, use, sharing, storage and maintenance.

In addition to legislation being a catalyst for compliance in relation to information management, let us not forget the impact of the political agenda. Here the public sector is under increasing pressure (from tax payers and the general public) to be more transparent in reporting activity and associated expenditures. Individuals are seeking greater access to data and information on which decisions have been based on a very wide range of policy initiatives in areas such as local planning, hospital closures, education, health and transport; and individuals are seeking access to their personal and medical records.

Governments themselves have played a part, promoting 'joined up thinking' and encouraging agencies to share and use information effectively. Sometimes this means dealing with very sensitive information held, for example, by social services, health services and the police.

High-profile enquiries such as the 9/11 Commission in the USA and the Bichard Inquiry in the UK raised questions about how information was stored, shared and deleted, as well as giving consideration to good information management practice. In this connection, one could also cite the work of the Truth and Reconciliation Commission in South Africa, as that inquiry focused on extracting information from many witnesses and used as a key 'incentive' the possibility of amnesty for abuses committed during the apartheid era.

One of the biggest growth areas for consultancy services has been in the financial area, where new compliance regulations are introduced with great regularity. Most challenging has been the introduction in the US of the Sarbanes-Oxley Act (2002), which affects not only US publicly quoted companies but also any company with a US connection. Companies are required to comply with a set of prescriptive, and some would say burdensome, rules to ensure investor confidence and prevent accounting fraud. Companies affected are required to submit an annual report of the effectiveness of their internal accounting controls to the Securities and Exchange Commission (SEC).

Since 2001 we have also seen the introduction by the International Accounting Standards Committee of international accounting standards, where a single set of global accounting standards, the International Financial Reporting Standards, seek to converge accounting standards across the world. The Basel II Accord is another example of the creation of an international standard, aimed at banks and their capital adequacy ratios. In the EU anti-money laundering directives applicable not only to the financial services sector but also to other key services where large cash transactions may be a feature of business activity (such as lawyers, accountants, estate agents, casinos and trust companies) continue to affect the way that information is recorded and reported to the appropriate authorities.

Some of the better-known regulatory bodies include in the UK the Financial Services Authority (FSA), the Charity Commission and the Health Protection Agency (HPA), and in the US the above-mentioned SEC, the Environmental Protection Agency and the Food and Drug Administration. All monitor activities and adherence to compliance in their particular industries and sectors.

In India, regulatory compliance lags behind that seen in Europe and the US, with only about 20 per cent of companies implementing regulatory compliance programmes. However, as those responsible for compliance recognise the protections it affords and how instrumental it can be when trying to do business in the developed world, this percentage is improving. An example that highlights the improving regulatory environment is that any Indian or international company doing business with Indian companies has to comply with the Indian Information Technology Act 2000. This Act also updated the India Evidence Act, which now deals with evidence related to electronic records and their admissibility. Such records must be properly maintained, stored and reproduced in order to be admissible under the Evidence Act.

While China has yet to bring in wide-ranging regulatory compliance laws, as its economy grows and opens up to the rest of the world, the matter will no doubt be addressed. At present, the complex nature of relationships between local, national and federal laws in China is somewhat of a stumbling block to implementing country-wide regulation.

Organisations around the world want to be recognised as managing their information well and being compliant; they strive to adhere and be certified to international standards such as ISO 27002 Information Security and ISO 15489 Records Management.

The compliance demands on organisations are complex; they are not the same for every organisation and this only complicates the issue. There is little doubt that one of the biggest challenges facing organisations today is 'How do we make sure that we are compliant?'

The compliance challenge

The first step for any organisation is to make sure that it understands the compliance requirements in its particular industry or sector and what records it needs to keep. In this regard it may be necessary to seek expert advice and consult legal advisors, who should be able to provide full details of the legislative regimes applicable to the organisation.

Auditors can also provide guidance, particularly with regard to financial compliance, and an IT services provider may also be able to offer useful advice, particularly where technology solutions will play a role in meeting the challenges of information storage, retrieval, accessibility and reporting.

Government departments will provide advice and guidance to organisations in the public sector.

Once it has been established which regulations, standards and policies are applicable to the organisation it will be necessary to embark on a programme of activities to ensure that compliance issues are being dealt with effectively and that, if ever challenged, the organisation can defend its position and satisfy its regulators or a court of law.

Senior management

As with any major organisational initiative, it is important to get the board of directors and/or senior management to champion and promote the issue of information management compliance. Indeed, if there is already senior-level responsibility for the management of information assets, it should then be a logical next step for the same level to take ultimate responsibility for compliance.

Larger organisations will, in all likelihood, appoint a Compliance Manager (or similar) to take operational responsibility for compliance issues. In fact, in some organisations there are compliance teams whose duties focus on providing advisory services, offering guidance on related matters and performing internal audits to check on progress and accuracy in relation to compliance issues.

Developing policies and strategies

It will be appropriate to develop policies and strategies for information management compliance, with the aim of ensuring that all relevant statutory and legal obligations are met. Formal guidance ensures that every employee who needs to know is aware of the correct procedures to follow and is in no doubt as to the consequences of failing to comply with prescribed practices.

Employees should be clear as to what the specific statutory regulations are, who is responsible for which areas, what has to be done, what must not be done and the timescales involved. Any new legislation, rules and regulations usually have a timeframe attached to them, placing a responsibility on organisations to ensure that they can demonstrate compliance by a specified date. In most instances, compliance will be an ongoing matter and will have to be monitored constantly.

Policies and strategies will need to be applied consistently. This will not only create internal confidence in the operation of compliance regimes but will also instil confidence in the minds of external stakeholders. No organisation will want to see a repeat of the Arthur Andersen situation, where clients severed their association with the firm because of shortcomings in its management of information.

It is not possible to be prescriptive about the kinds of policies and strategies an organisation needs to develop and implement in the context of information compliance, but some general guidance can be provided.

At a minimum, an organisation needs to establish what information should be kept and for how long it should be stored and protected. This applies to information in paper and electronic formats, voice and instant messaging. Guidance as to retention periods needs to be clear. How long should information be kept? Does a statute of limitations apply? You may be required by law to retain certain records for a specified period of time.

Information should be capable of being retrieved in a timely fashion. As an example, in the UK, under the Freedom of Information Act 2000, a response to a request for information should be provided within 20 working days of receipt of the request. In Australia, the Freedom of Information Act 1982 stipulates that a request for information should be dealt with within 45 days of receipt.

Consider information security issues, and who may have access to what level of information. Not all information should necessarily be available to everyone in the organisation. Introduce strategies to ensure that access to information is recorded and that an audit trail can be provided to indicate who has been able to access what information.

E-mail and internet policy

Most organisations these days will have an e-mail policy as well as an internet usage policy. These policies will form part of the overall information management compliance policies and strategies.

E-mails constitute a formal record and may be used as evidence in the event of litigation, court proceedings, industrial tribunals and so forth. They may also be used as records for audit purposes. It is important for all employees to understand the potential implications of sending (and receiving) e-mails; if an appropriate policy is in place this will help to prevent any improper use.

Each e-mail account, whether a personal or group account, should normally be password protected and employees, unless the circumstances are exceptional, should not usually be able to access each other's e-mail accounts. Policy guidelines should comment on any exceptions to such a rule. Most e-mail policies will outline guidelines for creating e-mails and may include advice on the suggested layout, format and language to be used. Instructions as to the inclusion of disclaimers at the end of e-mails should be provided (if appropriate).

Guidance in respect of e-mail management should be provided so that there is consistency throughout the organisation. Details as to security and confidentiality should be conveyed and employees should be made aware of the importance of retaining e-mail records. Ideally, with the technologies now available, a system should be in place whereby records are archived automatically after a certain period of time, thus helping to ensure that nothing is deleted in error.

Training employees to recognise 'spam', hoaxes, scams and e-mail chain letters may form part of the e-mail policy.

There may be a restriction on using business e-mail for personal purposes and, if so, this should be stated in the policy. The penalties for e-mail abuse and misuse should be clearly articulated so that employees know the potential consequences.

As with other types of information, all data stored on organisational computer networks is the intellectual property of the organisation, not of the individual.

There is no doubt that the internet has had many benefits in business and that accessibility to information at the touch of a button has improved communications for all stakeholders, reduced costs and streamlined many activities. Yet there are concerns about misuse of the internet, so it is advisable to have an internet usage policy so that everyone is clear as to what is and is not acceptable.

Internet usage policies should make clear what the internet may and may not be used for: which sites are permitted, and which prohibited and whether or not the internet may be used for personal purposes. Policies should indicate what type(s) of internet activity will be monitored and what forms of surveillance will be used.

Security issues will be a very important part of the internet policy (passwords, privacy, use of virus scanning and firewalls, data encryption processes); anyone who tries to circumvent the security processes will in all likelihood face disciplinary action, and this should be made clear in the policy document.

Formulating strategies and policies may involve obtaining professional advice from lawyers, accountants, bankers or regulatory bodies to ensure that nothing has been overlooked. Because it is a rapidly changing area, with guidance being regularly reviewed and updated and new regulations being passed, it is important to keep a watch on what is happening in your particular industry or sector so as to ensure that compliance requirements are always addressed appropriately.

Responsibility for information management compliance

As mentioned, larger organisations may have a member of staff whose role includes all aspects related to ensuring that the organisation is compliant. This may include reporting directly to a member of the board on compliance issues as well as driving forward formulation of organisational strategy and policy in this area. However, all the responsibility does not fall on one person (the Compliance Manager or similar), and everyone in the organisation has a role to play.

The level of individual responsibility and what is expected of personnel should be made clear in policy documents, so that all employees are aware of and understand compliance requirements in relation to their particular roles, responsibilities and activities and how they, in turn, support the organisation's responsibilities.

Most commentators would agree that it is not sufficient merely to advise employees what to do and then expect them to do it. Advice and guidance needs to be accompanied by clarification as to what performance standards are expected; and reporting processes and mechanisms need to be in place to facilitate monitoring. It may be sensible to put in place a scheme involving rewards/penalties.

Appropriate systems and structures can create an environment where good information management compliance is part of the organisation's culture. In the final analysis, the onus for ensuring compliance will rest with individual employees, who should be ready and able to act in accordance with the established compliance frameworks. This requires leadership, training and a culture of trust and openness in the organisation. It is not suggested that this is likely to be an easy task – quite the contrary, given the complexity of today's operating environment. But non-compliance is not an option.

Training and awareness

As with any organisational change programme, it is important to provide training and education in compliance issues. Staff induction programmes should include a session on compliance and ongoing training will be needed, not least because of the continuing proliferation of new regulatory frameworks.

Depending upon the prevailing situation, compliance training may include:

- Awareness of the regulations affecting the organisation, whether legislative, regulatory or internal. In most instances organisations will be required to fulfil all three types.

- Awareness of whether the organisation's activities are subject to regulatory control by an overseeing body.

- Awareness of which types of information, both structured and unstructured, constitute records. These will include both the obvious and the not so obvious, such as e-mail, voicemail, instant messages.

- Policies on information and records creation, retention and destruction.

- Technology and software programmes available to support information management compliance.

- Applicable international standards, such as ISO 27002 and ISO 15489.

- Guidance on corporate responsibility and how to conduct business in an ethical manner; clarification on acceptable standards of behaviour.

- Sharing of good practices in information management compliance.

- Awareness of the consequences of failing to comply with the legislation, regulations and internal rules that affect the organisation.

If an organisation were challenged on any aspect of information management compliance, one question to be asked might relate to training. The organisation would need to provide evidence that appropriate structures were in place to ensure that employees were trained in this key area. 'Not knowing' about the regulations would be insufficient defence to avoid any penalty.

The area of compliance (and corporate governance) is a moving target; needs will change, new rules and regulations will be introduced, existing regulations will be updated and technology will advance, making compliance training something that requires regular attention and continual support.

Monitoring

Having established policies and delivered training, the organisation needs to monitor that the required actions are being taken. It will be necessary to establish processes to monitor what is happening and take early action to stem any shortcomings. That way, an organisation can be confident that it is meeting its compliance requirements.

Monitoring can be undertaken by either an internal or an external agent. It is perhaps stating the obvious to say that the personnel who do the monitoring should be qualified and experienced in compliance matters and knowledgeable in all related aspects – legal, technical, technological and organisational processes.

Monitoring may be done either selectively or on a full and detailed basis. Routine inspection is one option; alternatively, an inspection may be made when there is some cause for concern, perhaps as a result of a complaint or in the anticipation of legal proceedings.

Inspections may vary from a 'spot check' to a full inspection covering all parts of the organisation.

- *Spot checks* can be accomplished by a 'walk through', in which the monitoring person(s) reviews activities by observing practices and adherence to specified procedures, shadowing specific employees and observing how they manage information and whether or not they are complying with the guidelines.

- *Sampling* involves the monitoring person(s) reviewing a selection of records to ascertain whether they are compliant.

- *Full inspection* is the most time- and resource-intensive and will involve a thorough review of all information and records, interviews with employees, an examination of processes and procedures, and collection of any evidence of non-compliance.

It might be a good practice for the organisation to instigate a compliance audit of itself. This might be best done by a party that is external to the organisation, that has appropriate qualifications and that can offer an objective view. The company's auditors may provide such a service.

When an organisation instigates monitoring activities the following points need to be considered:

- How will the appropriate type of inspection be selected (spot check, sampling, full)?

- If it is not to be a full inspection, which parts of the organisation will be spot checked or sampled? On what grounds will they be chosen?

- What type of information and records will be reviewed – electronic, hard copy or both; structured, unstructured or both?

- How often should monitoring occur?

- Who should do it?

- Will the monitoring activity be overt or covert? Will employees receive prior warning or not?

Some organisations may be comfortable with simply asking employees to self-monitor and self-certify, at regular intervals, that they are observing and adhering to compliance requirements. For other organisations nothing other than a formal and thorough review by qualified personnel will be acceptable.

Compliance – burden or opportunity?

Compliance emphasises the need for the organisation to be transparent and accountable for its actions; regulators want to see evidence of suitable processes and procedures and confirmation that they are being followed.

Many organisations have initially viewed compliance as a burden: the large amount of legislation and regulation has placed the onus upon organisations to demonstrate that they are compliant and the regulations appear to focus on the penalties of non-compliance rather than on showing how compliance may actually present opportunities to improve business operations.

Of course, there are organisations whose response to the regulatory environment has been to do the minimum possible – maybe introducing some new technology to help automate some processes – and who generally see compliance purely as a 'box ticking' exercise to satisfy the regulators, and nothing more.

Forward-thinking organisations will view compliance as something that can really improve operational activities and add value to the business. The requirement to comply with regulations can be a catalyst for changing the way an organisation operates. By streamlining processes and making them more consistent throughout, by standardising procedures and integrating technologies for more efficient working, the organisation can strengthen itself.

Examples of some of the opportunities presented by compliance are given below.

E-mail

There have been a many cases of corporate scandal involving the inadequacy of e-mail records, and courts have imposed fines where a party has been unable to produce evidence in the form of relevant e-mails. These instances have prompted other organisations to review carefully their own e-mail policies and to establish procedures clarifying what may and may not be done with e-mail, what e-mail records should be kept, how they should be maintained and, importantly, what e-mails may safely be destroyed without fear of reprisal in the event of court or tribunal proceedings at some future date.

Technology

Compliance has been a driver for the integration of technologies, leading to lower operating costs over the medium and the long term. Duplication has been reduced and activities streamlined. In the financial services industry, for example, many businesses have seen compliance as an opportunity to integrate their customer records, thereby providing 'a single view of the customer'. Consolidating information enables any employee dealing with a specific customer, whether face-to-face in the local branch, by telephone in a call centre or via the internet, to have immediate access to the full records and thus to offer the right products and services to the customer at the right time. Good customer relationship management has been a by-product of information management compliance.

Regulatory information

While it may be burdensome to provide information in a specified format to satisfy the regulators, the forward-thinking organisation has seen this as an opportunity to review how it uses information and whether it could be used in more innovative ways and to much better effect. Through improved analysis of trends and customer behaviour, opportunities have been taken to review and develop more effective sales and marketing strategies, leading to improved performance.

Investor confidence

By having to comply with stricter financial reporting standards, companies producing annual reports and accounts have seen investor confidence increase. The regulations have been successful in ensuring that there is now far less opportunity for corporate misdemeanour. The codes of conduct aimed at directors have improved corporate governance and instilled greater investor confidence in a business.

Freedom of Information (FOI)

UK public sector bodies faced significant challenges to prepare themselves for the implementation of the FOI Act in 2005. A precursor of the FOI Act was implementation of publication schemes whereby public authorities were required to make certain categories of information readily available to the public, thereby eliminating them from specific consideration under FOI. Making information 'readily available' meant making it accessible via websites, the government Stationery Office, through public libraries or on written request. This and the implementation of FOI have caused public authorities to recognise that the public responds positively to organisations that promote greater openness and greater public accountability.

The above are just a few examples of the opportunities that have been exploited as a consequence of compliance. While the initial reaction may be to see compliance as a burden that must be carried, these examples indicate how turning a potential burden into an opportunity can result in real business benefits.

Benefits of information management compliance

Good information management compliance enables an organisation to see what it does well, to identify where it is not complying so well, and where it needs to improve. While compliance is often viewed negatively and felt to be tying up valuable resources that could be better used elsewhere, there are many operational benefits, aside from the obvious one of avoiding fines and penalties, that accrue as a result of good information management compliance, as described below.

Managing information as an asset

Compliance requires an organisation to know what its information assets are, to understand how and where they are stored and how employees are able to access them. We have seen in Chapter 3 the importance of regarding information as an asset that requires careful management. If your organisation has followed the suggested guidelines and identified the different types of information assets it uses, it is much better placed to maintain ongoing operations. The use and application of these information assets is essential to wealth creation and revenue generation in the information economy.

Faster decision making

Information management compliance encourages organisations to adopt a structured approach to classifying and storing information. This creates consistency and means that employees know where to look for decision-critical information and have ready access. They do not have to spend inordinate amounts of time trying to locate important information.

Improved communication

By having to implement compliance practices and procedures across the organisation in order to meet regulatory requirements, different business departments have to work together to ensure consistency in the compliance processes, that duplication is avoided and that any potential for conflict is addressed. Encouraging different parts of the organisation to work together on compliance issues opens up new communication channels that can also be used in other business initiatives and activities.

Using collaborative technologies to support compliance activity opens up opportunities for information sharing in other fields and across time zones and geographical locations.

Information security

Concerns about identity theft and security of personal information have emerged as key consumer issues. Organisations that can demonstrate increased and improved information security through compliance activity are better able to satisfy customers' concerns about the way their personal information is handled, and may even gain a competitive edge in doing so.

The security and privacy issues addressed by compliance have reduced the incidence of security breaches, but organisations must remain vigilant. Compliance has prompted organisations to consider seeking certification to international standards such as ISO 27001 and ISO 27002 (Information Security Management Standards). An organisation will increase consumer confidence by obtaining these certifications, as the standards demonstrate to the world that private and confidential information is being managed appropriately.

ISO frameworks

Obtaining certification against ISO standards and frameworks as part of a compliance initiative provides consistent security controls and instils both customer and investor confidence. We have mentioned the Information

Security Management Standards; organisations are keen also to obtain certification under ISO 15489, the Records Management Standard.

ISO certifications can also help in the case of the 'due diligence' reports required prior to a merger or takeover. When the acquiring company can see that there is good adherence to controls, it will know that the eventual integration of activities and systems will be much easier to manage.

When business partners and suppliers have similar procedures in place, activities can be streamlined and relationships enhanced.

Protection against fraud

The regulatory environment in which today's organisations operate has arisen partly as a protection against fraud. Information security controls help to protect against IT fraud, and many of the financial reporting regulations help to guard against financial fraud. Financial scandals such as Enron should be averted in future through effective compliance.

Defence against legal action

The very fact that an organisation has robust compliance procedures in place can give significant weight to the defence in a legal action for, say, a breach of confidentiality. Courts and tribunals will look more favourably on organisations that can provide evidence of compliance and can show an information audit trail in support of their defence.

Some organisations may initially view compliance as an unnecessary administrative burden and a financial drain on the business, but the reason why an increasingly onerous regulatory environment has developed is that there were shortcomings, sometimes very significant ones, in the ways businesses operated. Compliance should be viewed as a tool that can really help a business to operate more efficiently, and as offering protection in a variety of areas.

Ideally, compliance activities should become embedded in day-to-day operations rather than being considered unnecessary and onerous.

Poor information management compliance

Poor information management compliance can lead to litigation, financial penalties and even imprisonment. The risk of loss of reputation and investor confidence keeps many organisations alert to any shortcomings in compliance: no one wants to be the next 'Enron' and see their business fail as a result of poor or inadequate attention to compliance issues.

Compliance is compulsory: there is no opting out of compliance. It is not new, in the sense that organisations have always had to comply with regulations; but what is new is the increasing complexity of compliance and the growing demands this places on businesses.

Compliance can certainly be costly, but the costs of non-compliance can be even higher. It is not something that can be regarded as a one-off exercise; it requires ongoing attention and must become part and parcel of daily operations.

Organisations that weave compliance into daily activities and regard it as an integral part of doing business will be ensuring that their business is operating in a consistent manner, safely, fairly and objectively, and with minimal risk to all its stakeholders (employees, customers, suppliers, investors) and to the industry as a whole, and it will be confident that legal and regulatory demands are being satisfied.

Summary

In this chapter we have considered information management compliance, which has become a business-critical issue, especially since organisations now have to operate in an increasingly regulated environment.

The quantity of legislation, regulations and internal guidelines has posed many challenges, not least in getting organisations to ensure that business processes and reporting standards are robust and can satisfy any level of scrutiny by regulatory bodies. Regulators will want to see evidence that an organisation is operating within the relevant laws and regulations – that it is compliant; that an organisation has processes in place to ensure that it is observing the laws and regulations – that it remains compliant; and that, if called upon, an organisation can prove retrospectively, via its record keeping, that it has observed the laws and regulations – that it can demonstrate compliance.

To ensure compliance, an organisation must first find out which laws, rules and regulations are applicable to it and then develop consistent and robust policies to meet those requirements. Responsibility should be delegated to appropriate personnel. No one can escape the need for compliance, so make sure that suitable and ongoing compliance training is given to employees. Monitor activities and ensure that mechanisms are in place to address promptly any compliance shortcomings.

Rather that viewing compliance as a costly burden to be endured, consider it in a positive light and think of the opportunities and benefits it can bring to your organisation: consistency of processes, better communication, faster decision making, protection against fraud and misdemeanour, a safer working environment and enhanced reputation.

Do be clear about the potential risks and make clear to all employees how and why they may be personally liable if they fail to comply. Regulators have many powers to impose penalties and can even, in some circumstances, sell a business to another party that has demonstrated that it is compliant.

Make sure that your organisation can demonstrate compliance and can stand up to any in-depth scrutiny by legal and regulatory bodies.

Toolkit activity

■ Activity 12: Are you compliant?

9

The role of the chief information officer

Introduction

Growing recognition of the importance of information has led many organisations to initiate activities that allow information to be managed as an asset and exploited for competitive advantage. We have seen throughout this book the range of activities that need to be undertaken if information management is to fulfil its promise by becoming a reality and taking its place at the heart of organisational activity.

Many organisations have created new roles in the area of information management. We have seen the emergence of positions with the title of Chief Information Officer (CIO) or similar names such as Director: Information Management; Information Services Manager; Corporate Information Manager; Business Information Manager; Information Architect.

While a variety of titles exist, fundamentally, the incumbents in all these roles are tasked with responsibility for instigating, maintaining and monitoring information management activities. Having someone in a senior position to lead the information management programme sends out a message that information is seen to be important to the whole organisation.

Irrespective of the title, the role seems to be regarded from either a technology perspective or a management perspective.

In the former the emphasis is on the management of technology-based information systems, whereas in the latter the emphasis is much wider and attention is given to information in its broadest sense and its integration with other aspects of organisational activity.

If the technology perspective, rather than the integrative perspective, dominates, the challenge of embedding information management throughout the organisation is much more demanding. The interrelationship between technology and information management is undoubtedly close; however, technology should be the enabler of information management rather than the driver. With this in mind, this chapter will focus on the CIO role from an integrative perspective and consider the skills and attributes required in this broader context.

Recruiting a CIO

When creating the new role of CIO, give thought first of all to the job profile. This should clarify the following details.

Title

Give careful thought to the title and make sure that it reflects the role. It is not uncommon to see titles created haphazardly, without considering the real meaning of the role. Use the language of the organisation. For example, if senior managers are referred to as Executives or Chiefs, then reflect this as appropriate in the title of the position.

Reporting line(s)

To whom will the CIO report? In the minds of many organisations the CIO role is inextricably linked with information technology. Is there a Chief Technology Officer or equivalent? To whom does that person report and should the CIO have a similar reporting line? Should the CIO have oversight of information and communication technologies, so as to ensure that they do not conflict with the task of information management? What level of seniority will the CIO role have and where will it fit in the overall hierarchy? Will the CIO report to or be a member of the board of directors?

Purpose

Why is the role being created and how will it add value to the organisation?

Key accountabilities

Different organisations will place importance on different aspects of the role, depending upon how they see information management adding value to the business. An example of a job profile for a CIO is provided in Box 9.1.

Box 9.1   Chief information officer job profile

Title: Chief Information Officer

Reports to: Director of Operations

Purpose: To be responsible for instigating, maintaining and monitoring information management activities to ensure that the organisation remains competitive in its chosen marketplace.

Key accountabilities:

The CIO role will be challenging, combining change management, strategy, planning, implementation and relationship building. The role requires an individual with a keen interest in excellence, an ability to think strategically and to introduce and lead change in a complex environment.

Accountabilities:

- Set the strategic direction for information management in order to facilitate information sharing and effective application of collaboratively created information within the organisation
- Ensure that information management activities are proactively linked to strategic business objectives and support business needs
- Maximise the use of information resources, with particular emphasis on ensuring that information is available to the right people, in the right place, at the right time and in the right format
- Ensure that information sharing is embedded in the culture and processes of the organisation
- Actively lead and manage projects relating to information management and identify organisational training needs
- Actively keep abreast of new developments in the area of information management through a network of internal and external contacts, and by attending professional meetings, conferences and seminars.

After you have compiled the job profile, the next step is to create a person specification based on the job profile and to consider the skills, attributes and qualifications that the post holder will need in order to perform effectively. These should be categorised under two headings: those that are essential and those that are desirable. 'Essential' means skills that any candidate *must* have, that are a 'need to have', and 'desirable' means those skills that are 'nice to have'. A way to distinguish between the two is to consider how the job would be affected if the post holder did not have a specified skill, attribute or qualification. What difference would that make to good job performance? If it would have a detrimental effect, then that skill/attribute/qualification must go into the 'essential' category.

General observations on the CIO role

There is no generic job description applicable to a CIO, and the role varies from one organisation to another. However, for most it will involve full participation as a member of the senior management team. Thus, a range of skills will be central to effective performance. The role, especially if it is a start-up position, will be challenging, but potentially very rewarding. The opportunity to make a real contribution and difference to organisational success is what inspires many CIOs to achieve excellence.

People from a range of organisational and professional backgrounds have made a successful transition to a CIO role, not least because they understand the organisational complexities and also have proven themselves to be capable change agents who are able to engage the support of the whole workforce in fulfilling the information management agenda. Their backgrounds may be in business, in information and communication technologies, or in the information/library profession. Some come to information management through a change of career path (often after taking a study break to gain relevant qualifications); some find that their initial role in an organisation is expanded to incorporate responsibility for information management.

When appointing a CIO an organisation needs to ask what exactly it wants of that person. Does it want an expert? Is this the ideal solution for the organisation? If the CIO is to participate as a full member of the senior management team and in a multi-functional leadership role, where should their expertise lie? If the role includes change management and knowledge management in addition to information management and information technology, where should the balance of specialism lie?

Some of the first forays into information management made the mistake of assuming that if technology were made available, that alone would address the issues. Early advocates of information management focused too heavily on a specialism in IT, often to the detriment of the wider organisational agenda of information management.

If the CIO is expected to deliver organisational change through information management, the emphasis should be on expertise in leading change programmes. Getting organisational buy-in to information management will mean that the CIO also needs to demonstrate an ability to manage across different functional and operational groupings.

A CIO needs to have credibility, and this can come only from personal and professional attributes and record. However, if the CIO role is a new one it may be impossible to import credibility, so you will need to seek evidence that the successful candidate has not only initiated and led change agendas, but also has previously demonstrated an ability to engage others in innovative practice and new ways of working and has a professional and educational background that indicates the required competencies.

A single CIO placed primarily to act as a catalyst for organisational change will be somewhat different from a CIO operating in a clearly defined and structured role. The start-up role may evolve into the second type of role, and the question then arises whether both kinds of role require a similar portfolio of skills.

In a start-up CIO role a 'charismatic innovator' is often the best bet. This is someone who has a keen interest in change and an acute political sense of how to negotiate through existing organisational structures. The role is primarily to lead the change agenda, to persuade and enthuse a wide constituency, and to make linkages to key operational areas so as to achieve some information management 'quick wins'. Experience has shown that such roles can be time limited: the keenness displayed in a start-up role may not be matched by willingness to be involved in the (possibly more mundane) longer-term role.

Key skills of CIOs in start-up positions

The scope of the CIO role will differ from organisation to organisation, and while a broad range of skills could be included in the person specification, the focus of this section is on the *key* skills required of CIOs in start-up positions.

Change management

In most cases the successful change manager is someone who manages in a participative way by involving the workforce, keeping it fully informed and encouraging it to adopt a positive attitude to new proposals. A good change manager will establish structures and processes to plan and manage an orderly implementation of change.

Understanding that everyone responds to change in an individual way, showing empathy and dealing tactfully with concerns and resistance will help to manage the processes constructively.

In many respects, one could justifiably argue that all of the following skill requirements are necessary in a change manager, rather than being skills required specifically of a CIO.

Leadership

Leadership involves taking responsibility for tasks, giving direction, providing structure and delegating tasks to others to get the job done. Leadership is more intangible than management and is the process of taking people in a particular direction and influencing them to produce an outcome.

Planning and implementation

This involves being able to set priorities, define targets and allocate responsibilities to others, as well as planning work so that results are achieved on time and within budget.

Communication

Communication involves developing interpersonal relationships, building alliances and persuading doubters. Studies in which CIOs have been work-shadowed indicate that a very high proportion of their time is spent communicating. Despite the range of electronic communication methods now available, it is face-to-face communication that dominates.

In order to gain organisational buy-in to information management a CIO needs to have the charisma to carry any sceptics and to be able to address firmly and clearly any concerns raised by employees.

Commitment

Displaying a real personal commitment to the task, and enthusiasm for what information management can deliver, will help the CIO to move forward the organisational agenda. The requirement for commitment is perhaps obvious, but the CIO does need to appreciate the potential scale of the challenge and how to address it, and to communicate this through words and deeds.

Negotiating skills

This means developing the ability to negotiate at all levels internally, and being able to negotiate effectively with external parties. The CIO must be able to articulate a view of 'where the organisation wants to be' and to negotiate from that standpoint – couching it first in terms of organisational results and improvements and then in specific information management terms. The key challenge is always to keep information management policies and strategies in alignment with desired organisational strategies and results.

Networking

Internal and external networking is an important aspect; a successful organisation-wide information management programme will ultimately have an impact on strategic and operational areas of the business. Externally, networking can be particularly valuable, especially in the early stages of an information management programme when the CIO may be the only person in the organisation who understands all the issues. Being able to network externally with peers, to share experiences and to learn from one another is invaluable.

Strategic awareness

This includes first, an understanding of the business and how it operates, its vision, mission and goals; and second, an understanding of how the organisation currently holds, uses, views and manages its existing information assets.

A CIO also needs to have a strategic awareness of the value of information and of how changes in the way organisational information is managed and used can help to improve business performance. An ability to identify and analyse knowledge flows across the organisation and to engage in process redesign activities will also be appropriate. Linked in to this is an ability to define and lead strategies for creating, using and archiving information in productive and meaningful ways that support business goals.

It is important for the CIO to understand the legal, regulatory and ethical environment within which information management must operate and to be cognisant of issues such as data protection, corporate governance, freedom of information, confidentiality, information security and privacy.

The CIO should demonstrate an awareness of the wider information management environment, interacting with communities outside the organisation and keeping up to date with new and developing trends in the field.

The CIO role and the IT debate

Successful information management projects focus on culture and processes ahead of technology issues. If the CIO is not a 'technology expert', then in order to be credible they must understand what information and communication technologies are available and how they serve the information management agenda.

A base-level knowledge of office systems, intranet, internet and extranet applications, and internal databases is necessary, as well as awareness of what information and communication technology tools can deliver. Keeping up to date with market developments and how new technologies can be employed to promote information management will serve a CIO well.

CIOs in established roles

CIOs in newly created roles have been likened to evangelists, selling and promoting the benefits of information management throughout the organisation. However, as information management becomes embedded in organisational practice the role of the CIO will evolve and develop. Many of the skills needed in a start-up CIO role will remain relevant in an established role, but there will be less need to spend time advocating the importance and relevance of information management and more time will be given to demonstrating successes and achieving tangible results.

A key task for the established CIO is to make sure that the information management programme maintains its visibility and momentum. As business environments change – and they do so with ever-increasing regularity – the CIO must consider how changes will affect information management and respond, if necessary, by restructuring and refocusing information management activity.

Effective information management undoubtedly poses many challenges for a CIO; the nature of those challenges will change, and the CIO who responds quickly to the changing environment will ensure that information management remains high on the organisational agenda.

Educational qualifications

Information management is now an accepted business discipline and organisations across the globe are creating roles for CIOs. Some organisations will be content for the CIO to build experience 'on the job' and by attending conferences and seminars and reading the literature; but for other organisations a professional qualification will be a requirement.

Employers seeking to recruit staff into a CIO role recognise that CIOs come from very diverse backgrounds. A professional qualification equips them with foundational skills, and also makes them better placed to meet the challenges presented by working in this demanding field.

Evidence suggests that a professional qualification in information management is of value. Building on the foundations of practical work experience, a professional qualification enables an individual to make the transition to a higher level of awareness in this discipline.

Universities around the world offer professional training and qualifications in information management at both undergraduate and post-graduate level. The latter seem to prevail, reflecting the senior level of people seeking appointment as CIOs.

Training courses

In addition to the degree-level programmes offered by universities, there are training providers who offer much shorter programmes in specialist areas. These range from foundation level to advanced level and cover a range of subjects, including information auditing, records management, copyright, content management and other information management-related topics.

Professional associations

Membership of a professional association such as the UK-based CILIP (Chartered Institute of Library and Information Professionals), the US-based IIMA (International Information

Management Association), the Indian Association of Special Libraries and Information Centres, or of less formal groupings such as networking forums or special interest groups, provides opportunities for CIOs to meet and share experiences. Many associations offer subscriptions to industry-based journals as well as staging regular conferences that provide not only the opportunity to learn and to discuss developments in the field, but also opportunities to network with peers around the globe.

Summary

In this chapter we have considered how, as a consequence of information management gaining attention, organisations have started to appoint individuals to lead the initiative, and we have seen that roles are being created with titles such as 'Chief Information Officer'. Such appointees are responsible for driving information management forward and have a key role to play as part of the senior management team.

For a newly created position, writing a job profile is the first step, followed by the development of a person specification. The latter will clarify those skills that are essential to the role and those that are merely desirable.

While a start-up CIO role differs somewhat from that of an established position, the key skills required remain fairly constant. Some organisations will insist on appropriate degree-level qualifications and, if this is the case, there are many academic institutions around the world that offer suitable programmes.

Membership of a professional association offers many benefits, not least the opportunity to keep abreast of new and emerging developments, but also opportunities for networking with peers.

The CIO role is a challenging one, particularly in a start-up situation, but the satisfaction of making a real contribution to organisational performance drives many CIOs to reap the rewards associated with success.

Toolkit activity

- Activity 13: Preparing for a chief information officer role

10

Concluding remarks

The material in this book is largely aimed at people in organisations where information management has yet to be established as a formal discipline. However, organisations that have embarked on their information management journey are not excluded, as the book has been written so that each chapter stands alone and can be 'dipped into' as circumstances permit.

I hope therefore that the content will appeal to a range of people with an interest in managing organisational knowledge, whether they are new to the subject or whether some elements of information management have already taken shape in their specific organisation. For those of us who have been working in this area for some time, it is beneficial to revisit the literature from time to time and reassure ourselves that what we are doing is in line with good practice.

There is little doubt that the world economy has changed, and that traditional sources of wealth – land, labour and capital – have been matched in importance by more intangible and intellectual resources such as information (and knowledge). Examine any publicly quoted company, and its market value typically exceeds its book value, the difference being attributed to 'intangibles' such as information.

The era of the information worker is now a reality and has prompted organisations to think very carefully about their information assets and how best to identify and manage them. Sophisticated information management techniques are driving competitive advantage.

Society has been managing information for thousands of years, but it is only since the mid 1990s that it has become an important area of focus for organisations and that information management has emerged as a formal business discipline.

Despite the documentation provided by case studies to highlight the importance of effective information management and its contribution to organisational success, some organisations are still somewhat reluctant to approve and proceed with information management initiatives. One of the major reasons for this is the perceived difficulty of establishing a sound business case for information management.

This book has aimed to demonstrate how information management activity should be at the heart of organisational activity and how the business case can be made in terms of its contribution to organisational success.

No information management programme should proceed on a stand-alone basis. Always make sure that it is clearly aligned with the wider business goals. Make an assessment of the organisation's strategy and business goals and use these as the foundation on which to build the case for information management. Identify and understand those business goals which resonate loudest with senior management.

By using established practices to form the business case and by identifying the options and weighing them against a 'do nothing' scenario, it should be easier to achieve support from senior-level management. Do not shy away from having to subject the investment in an information management programme to the same rigorous examination as would be applied to any similar request for resources. Establish metrics that will allow you to measure performance and demonstrate the benefits information management will bring throughout the organisation.

This book has adopted a pragmatic approach to information management and has attempted to present a logical framework that can be followed, at whatever stage of implementation you may be.

The book has not sought to comment on the technologies and applications that are available as enablers for information management. That would be a subject for another book in its own right (which would soon become out of date as the pace of innovation grows). However, we must not overlook the impact that developing technologies have had and continue to have on better management of information. Technology has provided tools with which to find, capture, organise, store and share information in ways that were never imagined by previous generations. Embrace technology as the enabler it so rightly is; but do not use it as a driver for information management. First and foremost consider culture and process, and then technology, as you roll out your programme.

I hope that by following the guidelines and frameworks suggested here you will be able to successfully justify the business case for information management and that your initiative will be an unqualified success.

Appendix
Strategic information management toolkit

The toolkit draws on the material presented in this book. It aims to provide practical assistance in the form of development activities and discussion topics that have been designed to help you enhance your strategic information management skills.

Not all of the activities may be relevant to your own individual situation, so use them selectively.

Activity 1: Developing strategic awareness

- Buy and read a strategy textbook to broaden your knowledge and use as a reference source. Suggested titles:

  - G. Johnson and K. Scholes, *Exploring Corporate Strategy: Text and Cases* (Financial Times/Prentice Hall, 2006).

  - G. Hamel and C. K. Prahalad, *Competing for the Future* (Harvard Business School Press, 1996).

- Find out the current corporate strategy and the top six key initiatives of your organisation.

- Find out which strategic tools and frameworks are used in your organisation and familiarise yourself with them.

- Talk to people who are involved in strategy formulation in your organisation about the processes that are used to formulate strategy.

- Examine internal documentation, past and current, and decide whether or not the strategies were/are being realised. If not, why not?

- Identify the ways in which your organisation's strategy depends on good management of information. Consider what information management strategies and policies you need to develop to support the corporate strategy.

- Analyse your organisation using some or all four of the tools outlined – SWOT, STEEPLE, Porter's Five Forces or Scenario Analysis.

- Talk to other managers in your organisation about current strategic issues.

- Read in depth about one or two particular strategic initiatives being pursued by the organisation and track their progress.

- Keep up to date by reading the business and professional press.

- Subscribe to a journal on strategy, such as *Strategic Management Journal*, *Long Range Planning* or *Sloan Management Review*.

- Join a professional business strategy forum such as The Business Strategy Forum (www.businessstrategyforum .com).

- Join an online discussion group covering strategic issues.

- Attend a strategy-related conference. Marcus Evans (www.marcusevans.com) hosts conferences on a wide range of topics including strategy; the Association for Strategic Planning (www.strategyplus.org/conference .shtml) holds an annual conference.

Activity 2: SWOT template

- Complete a SWOT analysis of your organisation from a general perspective (no more than five items in each quadrant).

- Do the same from an information management perspective. Where are the similarities and differences?

The simplicity of SWOT enables it to be used at any level in the organisation.

Strengths: (internal perspective)	Weaknesses: (internal perspective)
■ ■ ■ ■ ■	■ ■ ■ ■ ■
Opportunities: (external perspective)	Threats: (external perspective)
■ ■ ■ ■ ■	■ ■ ■ ■ ■

When completing a SWOT remember:

Strengths: What is the organisation good at? What (competitive) advantages can the organisation exploit?

Weaknesses: What impedes the achievement of goals? What do your competitors do better than you? What areas does the organisation need to develop? Which areas attract most negative feedback from customers?

Opportunities: These are features of the external environment that you may/should be able to exploit to advantage.

Threats: What might happen in the external environment to put your organisation at a disadvantage and hinder its competitive position?

Activity 3: STEEPLE exercise

Using STEEPLE in a small group, write down the key influences on your organisation (no more than five in each category) and then rate them using the grid below.

STEEPLE analysis factor	Impact (High/Medium/Low/Unknown)	Impact (+positive/-negative)	Importance (High/Medium/Low)	Notes
Socio-cultural				
Technological				
Economical				
Environmental				
Political				
Legal				
Ethical				

Doing this exercise in a group enables you to canvass a variety of views and stimulates debate about where the strategic priorities may lie. In strategic planning, it is often used in conjunction with SWOT analysis. The two complement each other well.

Activity 4: Defining information management

- How would you describe the current focus of information management in your organisation? Is it happening at all, or in isolated pockets with no overall coordination of activity, or is it an organisation-wide initiative?

- Think about how information is regarded in your organisation.

  - Is it helping to achieve organisational objectives?

  - What opportunities exist for promoting the concept of information management?

  - What can you do to help raise the profile of information?

- Using the following example of a set of sales figures, consider the continuum:

  $$Data \rightarrow Information \rightarrow Knowledge$$

  to analyse a work-related situation with which you are familiar.

Monthly sales figures are provided giving details of the level of sales in each product category – this is **data** (it must be interpreted to be useful).

The sales figures are compared against previous monthly trends – this is **information** (it has specific meaning in a given context).

You realise that poor sales figures for the latest month can be attributed to a computer breakdown that affected online sales levels – this is **knowledge** (it depends on insight and experience).

- Has your organisation implemented systems such as records management, electronic document management, customer relationship management, and/or an intranet?

  - Have the systems been implemented independently of each other or has a coordinated approach been taken?

  - If they have been implemented independently, where might it be possible to coordinate activities?

  - Whom would you need to involve in doing this?

- Discuss the concept of information management with work colleagues. People from different parts of the organisation will have differing perspectives, so invite a range of people to participate in the discussions.

- Read your organisation's annual report and/or other formal reports.

  - Do they refer to the importance of information?

  - Can you use this to raise the profile of information management?

Activity 5: Information as an asset

In the context of your own role and using the categories outlined in the Hawley Report, list the top three information assets that you have identified as being important and/or strategic. Ask your immediate colleagues to do a similar exercise and compare notes. This will generate debate and will help to clarify a common understanding of information assets.

Information assets by category	
Market and customer information	■ ■ ■
Product information	■ ■ ■
Specialist knowledge	■ ■ ■
Business process information	■ ■ ■
Management information	■ ■ ■
Human resource information	■ ■ ■
Supplier information	■ ■ ■
Accountable (i.e. compliance) information	■ ■ ■

- Put together a cross-functional team and do a similar exercise.
  - Where are the similarities and the differences in your perceptions as to the most important organisational information assets?
  - What does this say about your organisation?
- Make a short presentation to senior-level management about your findings and discuss what actions should be taken in light of your assessments.
- Think of a work-based decision you had to make recently. List the information assets used in making the decision, then evaluate each one on the following basis:

1 = Very valuable 2 = Valuable 3 = Moderately valuable 4 = Of some value 5 = Of no value

- Use a similar assessment and evaluation technique for a project that you were involved in.
  - What information assets did you use and how valuable were they?
  - Were any information assets unavailable and what impact did this have on the project?
  - What additional information assets would you want to have access to if working on a similar project in the future?
- If you work for a stock market-listed company, read the annual report and accounts, and in particular the narrative report.
  - Does it mention information assets? If not, discuss this with the company accountant and find out why.

- The narrative report should comment on a number of aspects including financial and non-financial key performance indicators (KPIs).

- Is there or should there be a KPI relating to the effective management of information?

■ Keep abreast of developments in accountancy reporting standards by reading relevant journals such as *Accountancy Age, International Journal of Accounting, Auditing and Performance Review, Journal of Accounting Research* and/or accessing websites. A good source of information is www.icaew.co.uk, which provides advice and guidance on International Financial Reporting Standards. Keep your eyes open for any new guidance with regard to the reporting and valuation of information assets.

Activity 6: Employing external consultants

If you are considering using external consultants to help you with the information audit, here are some questions that you should ask and satisfy yourself about.

- Have the consultants worked in your sector before?
  - Do they understand your operations, your markets and the environment in which your organisation operates?
- What scale of information audit have the consultants undertaken previously? (Their experience should be commensurate with the size and scope of your organisation's audit.)
- Can you obtain references from previous clients?
- Can the consultants provide examples of previous audit outcomes?
- What can/will the consultants supply in terms of results and reports?
  - You can specify what you want them to produce. Can they meet your requirements?
- How will their findings, conclusions and recommendations be presented?
  - You can specify exactly what you want. Can they meet your requirements?
- Are they linked to software suppliers? (Beware of consultants who may be on-selling additional services and products.)
- What skills/expertise does the consultant's audit team have?
  - Will it complement the in-house team?

- How will the consultants transfer their expertise and knowledge to organisation staff?
- Will costs and fees be within your budget? Are there any hidden 'extras?'

Activity 7: Questionnaire design

It is most important that the questions are well written –
respondents must stay interested! If they feel that questions
are supportive, objective and easy to answer, response rates
will be high and response bias will be minimised. Provide
answer choices that are likely to match respondents'
opinions or experiences. This will produce high-quality
data, the analysis will be relevant to the situation in your
organisation and the results will be more useful.

Give careful thought to the questions you write. Study
examples of questionnaires if possible, and refer to the
guidance below.

Always pilot your questionnaire and act on any feedback
you receive.

To decide whether questionnaires are appropriate consider:

- Is this the right data collection method for the purposes
  of the information audit?
- What information is needed?
- Who are the respondents?
- Have I sufficient resources for questionnaire administration?
- Have I sufficient resources for data analysis?
- Have I completed preliminary planning to understand
  fully what questions need to be asked?
- Are the questions worded clearly?

Types of questions – open and closed

Open questions allow the respondent to comment freely
without any constraint. They can be used to collect
qualitative material to supplement quantitative data. The
following are examples:

1. What are the most useful information resources you use?

2. Which business units do you find it difficult or impossible to obtain information from?

Closed questions must be drafted in such a way that respondent has to choose. They are less time consuming for the respondent to answer and easier to analyse than open questions. The following are examples of different types of closed question.

List questions

A choice of items is offered, any of which may be selected.

Please tick any of the following information sources that you use	
Newspapers	
Journals	
Library	
Information unit	
Intranet	

Which two of the following aspects of information resources are the most important to you and which two the least important?	Most important	Least important
Ability to find it quickly		
Being able to respond promptly to enquiries		
Availability of accurate information		
Availability of comprehensive information		
Choice of retrieval/delivery method		
On-site storage of hard-copy documents		
Internal Information Resource Unit		

Category questions

These are designed to elicit one answer from the respondent, which can fit only one category.

When reading documents do you prefer	
Hard copy	
Electronic copy	

Which office are you based in?	
London	
Birmingham	
Manchester	

How often do you visit the Information Resources Centre?	
Weekly	
Fortnightly	
Monthly	
Quarterly	
Six monthly	
Annually	

Ranking questions

Where the respondent is asked to put something in rank order. The list needs to be kept fairly short, otherwise respondents will have difficulty in ranking items.

Choose the top three and rank in order of importance. 1 = most important, 3 = least important	
Why did you choose to work for this organisation?	
Pay	
Job security	
Interesting work	
Training	
Flexitime	
Study leave for professional qualifications	
Senior gap year	

Scale questions

These are commonly used in attitude, belief or behavioural surveys, where respondents are asked to mark their response along a scale.

Please indicate the extent to which you agree or disagree with the view that the following are effective methods of sharing information in the organisation.	Strongly agree	Agree	Disagree	Strongly disagree	Don't know
Departmental meetings					
Business group meetings					
Newsletters					
Training seminars					
E-mail					
Word of mouth					
Intranet					

Yes/No questions

These are simple!

	Yes	No
Do you think that this organisation has a culture that encourages information sharing?		

Question-writing skills

Writing effective questions is a skill and no question is 'good' in all situations, but there are some good practices that will help you write constructive questions:

- Keep the language simple
- Keep the questions short
- Avoid double-barrelled questions. Include only one topic per question
- Avoid leading questions, e.g., 'Most people believe that information is an asset that needs to be managed. Do you agree?'
- Avoid negative questions if possible, e.g., 'Would you prefer not to use a non-electronic source?'
- Avoid complex questions. Break them down into their components
- Do not use hypothetical questions. These will receive hypothetical answers
- Avoid topics that may give offence, e.g., age, income, political issues
- Keep open-ended questions to a minimum.

Activity 8: The case for information management

- Consider the range of information sources and resources you need to do your job effectively. Are they always available to you in right information/right time/right place/right format model? If not, what adjustments would ensure that information is available in line with the model?

  - Ask colleagues to do a similar exercise and discuss your findings.

  - How can you use this to help build support for information management?

- Identify instances of processes or projects that did not go according to plan because of poor availability of information.

  - Involve colleagues in discussion and consider how matters might be improved.

  - You can use these examples to build your case for information management in the organisation.

- Learn about some information management success stories by:

  - subscribing to industry journals that feature case studies

  - attending information management-related conferences

  - joining discussion forums where information management success stories are shared

  - joining a professional association such as CILIP, ASLIB, AIIP, ARMA, all of which educate and train information professionals as well as providing networking opportunities to discuss issues.

- Try to create a Balanced Scorecard for your organisation, identifying how information management can help to achieve the business goals in all four areas of finance, customer relationships, internal processes, and learning and growth, and define a set of metrics to track progress. Remember that metrics should specify:
  - what or who is being measured
  - the target(s) to be reached
  - the timeframe for achievement

and that there should be no more than four or five in each of the four areas.

Activity 9: Understanding your organisation

- What is the organisation's vision?
- What is the organisation's mission?
- What values underpin the vision and mission?
- What are the organisation's key corporate goals?
- What type of culture prevails in the organisation?

Type of culture	✓
Power	
Role	
Task	
Person	

Determining the type of organisational culture will help you to identify whose support you need to enlist at an early stage so as to gain wide commitment to information strategy implementation.

- Whose support do you need? (The list of individuals may be quite comprehensive, depending upon the culture you have identified.)
- Discuss with work colleagues two recent instances of change in the organisation, one that was successful and one that was not successful.
  - Examine the reasons for success and failure.
  - What can you learn from this that will help you to gain organisation-wide acceptance for information policy and strategy?

Activity 10: Stakeholder analysis

This will enable you to identify allies (champions), spot potential areas of difficulty, and concentrate your efforts where they will have most effect.

1. Stakeholder map

- List all the people or groups who are likely to be affected by implementation of the information strategy.

- Draw stakeholder maps (one map per strategy). Write the information strategies in the centre and identify all the stakeholders according to their significance to the outcome of the change. Place those who are most significant nearest to the centre and those who are least significant at the periphery.

2. Influence/interest chart

Once you have identified the key stakeholders, plot their position on the grid below.

- Interest = who cares most about the outcome of the proposed change

- Influence = who can most affect the outcome of the proposed change

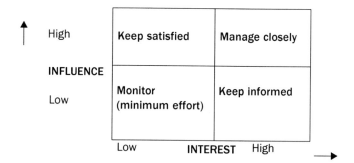

3. Consider each key stakeholder in turn and answer the following questions

- What are their priorities, goals and interests?
- How have they acted in the past?
- What specific action is expected of them in relation to the change (e.g., active support on specific tasks, willingness to work in a new way)?
- What is their attitude to the change? Are they likely to see it in a positive or negative light?
- What is their likely reaction? What issues might they bring up?
- What actions can you take in respect of this key stakeholder?

Plot the information of the following grid:

Stakeholder	Goals	Past reactions	Expected action	Change positive/ negative?	Likely reactions	Ideas for action

Activity 11: Developing information literacy skills

- A quick and easy way to evaluate whether a book is relevant to a topic on which you are searching for information is this four-step method:

  - Step 1: Look at the introduction, the final chapter and any abstracts. Scan the table of contents and read any testimonials printed on the front/back covers.

  - Step 2: Read the contents page, relevant chapters and chapter sections, and look at any tables and figures that have been used to illustrate points.

  - Step 3: Look at the index and read any topics of interest/relevance.

  - Step 4: Read the key points in the first and last paragraphs of each chapter.

- Locate two or three books on topics related to the type of work you do and use the above technique to consider what questions each book could answer.

- Ascertain which political party the various national newspapers endorse. Choose two papers that each support a different political party and read one article in each on the same politically related issue. Compare and contrast the articles, considering them for any political bias.

- Working with a colleague, choose an article from a scholarly journal. Review the article separately for content, style, coverage, bias, audience and language and then compare notes.

- Newspapers often carry articles that report on the outcome of original research.

  - Locate a newspaper article that comments on the results of original research.

- — Try to trace the original research findings. Consider the relationship between this and the article.
- — Has the research been reported accurately, or has the newspaper focused on a particular aspect or reported it out of context because it provides an attention-grabbing headline?

■ Locate a peer-reviewed scholarly journal article, a business journal article, a popular magazine article and a newspaper article all on the same topic and compare the articles to see whether there are any differences in the way the issues are presented.

■ In the context of either work or your personal life, identify an area on which you would like to expand your knowledge and understanding. Define the information needed to broaden your knowledge and understanding of it.

Activity 12: Are you compliant?

- Do you know which laws and regulations apply to your organisation? If not, do some research and find out. Is your organisation complying with them? If not, what needs to be done to ensure compliance?

- ISO standards 15489 (Records Management) and 27001 and 27002 (Information Security) will assist organisations with information management compliance. Obtain copies of the controls and frameworks and benchmark your organisation against them. Finding out what more your organisation needs to do to obtain ISO certification will enable you to see whether you need to strengthen activities in these areas. It may encourage your organisation to pursue ISO certification.

- Does your organisation have an e-mail and internet use policy? If not, discuss with your colleagues what you feel should be key standards for inclusion and consider drafting a suitable code of practice. Discuss how it might be implemented.

- Participate in any professional development activities that will enhance your understanding of compliance. Arrange to visit your industry regulators and learn what good practices can be introduced into your organisation.

- Instigate a mock regulatory compliance audit of your department and discuss the findings with colleagues. Consider how best to implement any recommendations made. This will help you to prepare for the full regulatory audit as well as helping to instil confidence in practices and procedures.

- Join and participate in industry compliance forums. Many industries have compliance forums where members meet to share experiences, good practices and current developments in the field. Some forums run annual conferences where peers can network in an informal setting. Other forums seek compliance-related articles for their publications. Could you write a compliance case study that would be of interest to other forum members? (Remember that you will need to obtain approval for publication from your organisation.)

- Subscribe to a compliance journal. There are general ones as well as journals that focus on specific industries, e.g., healthcare, IT, financial services.
- Volunteer to participate in any internal compliance projects.

Activity 13: Preparing for a chief information officer role

- Use the job profile outlined in Chapter 9 to create a person specification and decide what skills, knowledge and qualifications are necessary for good job performance, categorising them as either 'essential' or 'desirable'

Attribute	Essential ✓	Desirable ✓
Skills (e.g., change management) ■ ■ ■ ■ ■		
Knowledge (e.g., freedom of information legislation) ■ ■ ■ ■ ■		
Qualifications (e.g. master's degree in Information Science) ■ ■ ■ ■ ■		

- Imagine that you have set yourself a goal to be appointed to a CIO role. Draw up a personal SWOT analysis. This is a quick way to take stock of your own situation and analyse your readiness for such a role. Complete each of the four boxes, focusing on your work and life situations.

Strengths: (include personal qualities, skills, knowledge, experiences, support and resources) ■ ■ ■ ■ ■	Weaknesses: (include personal qualities, skills, knowledge, experiences, support and resources) ■ ■ ■ ■ ■
Opportunities: (focus on positives, include short, medium and long-term opportunities) ■ ■ ■ ■ ■	Threats: (include the barriers/obstacles that need to be overcome to achieve the goal) ■ ■ ■ ■ ■

- After completing the personal SWOT, develop an action plan to address the weaknesses and threats. Set a realistic timescale for achievement. Decide how regularly you will monitor progress toward your goals.

- Create a personal learning file. Record details of events that build your knowledge and experience in preparation for a CIO role. File materials such as useful articles, conference proceedings, any relevant presentations you have attended and any presentations that you have given. Keeping a record of what you have learned from each event, article, etc. and of how it will help you to achieve your goal will be very valuable to your personal development.

- Investigate the availability of relevant qualifications in information studies. Professional associations such CILIP in the UK and the American Library Association and the Australian Library and Information Association provide information on accredited undergraduate and post-graduate courses in information studies.

■ Investigate the availability of short courses in information studies. There are many training providers who offer suitable programmes. They are a useful means of quickly addressing any specific skills gaps that you have identified.

References, further reading and resources

Hamel, G. and Prahalad, C. K. (1996) *Competing for the Future*, Cambridge, MA: Harvard Business School Press.

Handy, C. (1993) *Understanding Organisations*, 4th edn, Harmondsworth, UK: Penguin.

The Hawley Committee (1995), *A Consultative Report: Information as an Asset: The Board Agenda*, KPMG IMPACT Programme.

Johnson, G. and Scholes, K. (2006), *Exploring Corporate Strategy: Text and Cases*, London: Financial Times/ Prentice Hall.

Kaplan, R. and Norton, D. (1992) "The balanced scorecard – measures that drive performance", *Harvard Business Review* (January–February), pp. 71–9.

Orna, E. (2004) *Information Strategy in Practice*, Aldershot, UK: Gower.

Porter, M. E. (1990) *Competitive Strategy*, New York: Free Press.

Schein, E. H. (1985) *Organizational Culture and Leadership*, San Francisco, CA: Jossey Bass.

Strassman, P. (1995) *The Politics of Information Management*, New Canaan, CT: The Information Economics Press.

Business Strategy Forum

Business Strategy Forum – www.businessstrategyforum.com.

Conferences and conference organisers

Association for Strategic Planning – www.strategyplus .org/conference.shtml.

Marcus Evans – www.marcusevans.com.

Journals

Sloan Management Review.
Long Range Planning.
Strategic Management Journal.

Index

Printed in the United Kingdom
by Lightning Source UK Ltd.
133957UK00001B/169/P